A Clubman at BROOKLANDS

By A C Perryman

ISBN 0 85429 251 9

First published June 1979

A FOULIS Motorcycling Book

Published by
Haynes Publishing Group
Sparkford, Yeovil, Somerset BA22 7JJ, England

Distributed in North America by:
Haynes Publications Inc.
861 Lawrence Drive, Newbury Park, California 91320, USA

Editor Jeff Clew
Layout design John Burnand and Alex Rollo
Dust jacket design Phill Jennings

Printed by: J.H. Haynes and Company Limited,
Sparkford, Yeovil, Somerset BA22 7JJ

Contents

Foreword

I little realised when I was asked by Bert Perryman to read through his manuscript that his chapters, as I read them, would bring back so many memories.

His early beginnings made me think of my own, which started with my first motor cycle, a Cedos. My father had promised it me if I became top of the class. In my case it was this that started it all.

I soon became a member of the famous Motor Cycling Club which was ruled over in those days by Mr. and Mrs. Marians (of loving memory). One of that club's major events was a high speed hour run at Brooklands track. I entered and began an association with a fantastic place and even more fantastic people. My mount was a 250 cc New Imperial and in 1926 I had the good fortune to make the fastest time in that class. I then proceeded to work on my Father, telling him that Brooklands was the place for us, to which he agreed. By 1928 we were established at Brooklands as the official track representatives for the New Imperial Company, carrying out all sorts of tasks for them, including world record attempts in the 250, 350 and 350 sidecar classes. My greatest accomplishment was riding the first 250 to establish a world record at over 100 mph.

1931 saw an ambition realised of becoming associated officially with the Velocette Company because their representative, Freddy Hicks, had left them to go to A.J.S. A much sought-after Brooklands 'Gold Star' became mine during my first race with a Velocette and lap records and wins over the different Brooklands circuits followed.

Mention by Bert of Len Heath in connection with his Ariel leads me to the Isle of Man, because in 1931 I went with Len to the Island on the *'Motor Cycle'* Senior Excursion and it was during this race that my very dear friend Freddy Hicks was killed. I was deeply shocked and in some way felt that I should try to conquer this course, so that in 1932 I was one of about 40 others mounted on new KTT Velocettes. Being the first Velocette home, in sixth position, started a long association with the Island which stretched on to 1948 with the entry of a New Imperial in the 250 class and a Velocette in the 350 and 500 classes.

My experiences have shown how, over the years, it is possible with good fortune to have many successes in the field of motorcycling.

Bert has made a number of references to the vehicles he used in taking his racing machines to many competitions, but I think that none had a stranger machine than my Father and I to get us to Brooklands in 1927 – a belt drive 4 1/4 hp Quadrant with a box sidecar. Later, it was replaced by a model T Ford van, which lasted for many years and was a source of much amusement.

I would hasten to congratulate Bert on the excellent way he has gathered all his racing experiences together and thank him for the opportunity I had of sitting back quietly and turning the clock back to the good old days. To me, there was nothing more humourous than when my twin sisters were made to ride round Brooklands on a 100 cc Atom Jap in 1930, the engine being the product of my good friend Teddy Prestwich of JAP Motors. The frame layout was the one I had used for motor cycle football many years before and was basically that of a Levis. My sisters broke world records with it, up to four hours. I slip in this anecdote to illustrate the sort of things which were done at Brooklands, particularly if there was some money in it. The girls had not yet reached fifteen and it gives me much pleasure in acknowledging my thanks to my sister Thelma, who has just typed this out for me.

4   L.J. Archer

Les Archer astride the 348 cc Velocette on which he won both the Junior and Senior Grands Prix at Brooklands on 29th July 1933. A month later he became the first man to cover 100 miles in an hour at a British track *(Motor Cycle)*

Acknowledgements

Many of the star riders of the day had their first taste of racing at the Clubman's Day Brooklands meetings. Names that flash through my mind, as I came into personal contact with them, are:- Noel Pope, Dave Whitworth, Johnny Lockett, and Dennis Loveday. There were doubtless many others. I never reached the heights in racing that the aforementioned attained, making only one appearance in the Island, and none anywhere else, because of financial limitations.

A lot of the names mentioned in these pages belonged to the 'lesser fry'. The 'big guns' are there, of course, but the more humble amongst the others, might also have aspired to feats of equal calibre, had they have had the opportunity.

This tale could not have been told without the help of others who were present at the time. Basil Keys, still racing after his first road race forty four years ago; worthy, I should think, of a place in the *Guiness Book of Records!*

Charles Mortimer, author of other stirring tales of Brooklands track. Les Archer, winner of more Brookland races than anyone else. Dr. Joe Bayley for supplying material from his immense stock of Brooklands records. Jim Lee, of the Vintage Motor Cycle Club. David McDougall, of Heath Bros. Garage at Frensham, for supplying race results of forty and more years ago.

My wife Connie, for her untiring efforts to get me to put pen to paper. Mrs Gill Budd for deciphering and typing my manuscript.

Mick Woollett, editor of *Motor Cycle Weekly*, for permission to publish quotes from *The Motor Cycle* and reproduce the fine action shots taken by that journal's photographers of the period.

John Pigneguy, who preferred to be known as 'J. Henry' as no one seemed able to correctly spell his name!, responsible for no less than three entirely different supercharged machines.

Lastly, Jeff Clew and my publishers; without them there would have been no book. I hope my readers derive as much pleasure in reading my story as I have had in compiling it.

Bert Perryman
Sompting 1978

About the Author

When he left school in 1928, Bert Perryman served an apprenticeship with the old London, Brighton and South Coast Railway at the Brighton Locomotive Works. At the same time he became interested in motorcycles, this latter interest forming the basis of this book. His love of the steam locomotive never deserted him and at the end of the war he joined a local model engineering society, determined to construct a steam locomotive of his own. One thing led to another and his most ambitious project by far was to construct a 5 inch gauge exact replica of 'Remembrance', the last locomotive built at the Brighton Works for the old LBSCR. With moves of house, the project took twelve years to complete and it has since proved a prize winner at numerous model engineering events, both as a runner and on static display. More recently, the author has constructed a second locomotive in conjunction with Lionel Woodhead, a 5 inch gauge Stroudley 'Gladstone' class locomotive which is much admired and took only two years to complete. Instrumental in re-forming the Worthing and District Society of Model Engineers, Bert was honoured by being appointed Chairman, a post he held for three successive years. He is now Vice President of the Society and confines his activities to making boilers and stationary steam models.

BROOKLANDS! What a magic word this was amongst the younger generation in the early years of this century. It was the first, and certainly the most famous of motor racing circuits in the world. To go there as a spectator was the wish of most young people of the day. To go as an actual competitor was regarded as the hallmark of a racing career, and something dreamed of by all young men (plus a few daring young ladies!) but accomplished by only a small minority of would-be aspirants.

One of the main reasons for this was, as always, cost. Motor racing has never been a cheap hobby and there were not the large sums to be had as prize money as is the case today. Sponsors were extremely rare, and one had to become very proficient to qualify for what was known as 'trade support'. There was a greater number knocking on the doors of the manufacturers of racing products, than the small band who had managed to make the grade at their own expense, thus qualifying for support of some sort or another.

This book is not intended to be a complete history of the famous track, alas no longer used for its intended purpose. Instead it is a factual year by year account of the striving of a young man of very modest means, to enjoy himself in the very exhilarating pastime of motorcycle racing. Car racing does not find a place in this tale. Firstly, I could not afford it; and secondly, I was not interested in it.

Undoubtedly the most sought after trophy in those years between the wars was a 'Brooklands Gold Star' presented to all members who lapped the outer circuit at a speed of 100 mph or over during a meeting. The first man to do so was the famous Herbert Le Vack in 1922 on a 1000 cc machine. A grand total of 183 Gold Stars were awarded between then and 1939 (when the track closed) and two 'Double Gold Stars' for a lap at 120 mph or over. A solitary 250 cc machine gained a Gold Star as long ago as 1933.

The Motor Cycle CLUBMAN'S DAY was inaugurated in 1932 for ordinary club members to try their hand on the track. With a coupon cut from that Journal, admission could be gained for one shilling, instead of the usual half-crown, and it was this concession that first sent me along and resulted in me being bitten by the 'Brooklands Bug'.

The following pages will describe the adventures that befell me during my seven years of racing at the famous track. I have tried to recapture the moments of extreme ecstasy, the bitter disappointments when things went wrong, and the trivial things, which several times robbed me of a first place when all was set for a win. I gained a lot of experience the hard way! I made many friends and found the majority of the contestants to be a grand body of men, who would go to great lengths to help you if they could.

Yes! I achieved my ambition; to win a 'Gold Star', and at my first attempt. That was one day when Lady Luck certainly rode with me. It made a splendid present for my 24th birthday.

8

Fighting for the lead in the 3rd September 1938 Junior Mountain Championship race at Brooklands. L.E. Brooks (12) glances at S.H. Goddard (19) as the latter draws alongside (*Motor Cycle*)

Chapter One

Early Days

The urge to travel at high speeds on two wheels was not born in me, as it was in many aces of the day. I only acquired it in my early twenties after I had sampled elementary competitive events organised by the local Brighton & District MCC which I joined in 1931, at the ripe old age of 19!

Upon leaving school at 16 I had only a very vague idea of how a petrol engine worked, but during that last summer holiday from school, my loving father of blessed memory presented me with a fifth hand, 1924 vintage, 350 cc side-valve New Hudson Sports model that he had persuaded the local milkman to detach from his milk-float sidecar, and part with for the princely sum of £5!

I soon found out quite a bit about petrol engines. You had to in those days, or else push the bike home! On an early sortie with father seated on the very high pillion seat, I misjudged a sharp right hander. The flint wall flanking the outside of the bend had a peculiar fascination for me, and to the chorus of 'you won't get round! you won't get round!' from astern, the New Hudson struck the wall a glancing blow and the whole equipage subsided in a cloud of dust! Luckily speed was very low and father had managed to plant his feet on the road and let the infernal machine get away from him. Junior suffered minor cuts and abrasions; the infernal machine now had bent handlebars and footrests, not to mention a sheared-off gear lever, but a hasty reconnoitre revealed that it might be rideable, with a bit of luck.

And so it proved to be. After we had recovered from the shock, I managed to persuade father to resume his elevated position astern and somehow managed to select second gear, which had to suffice for the entire homeward journey of some ten miles. The infernal machine was immediately interned in its shed, and the door locked. It was to remain so for the next fortnight. I had not been idle during this time though, and had managed to acquire a new gear lever.

Authority eventually relented, and with a shiny new gear lever and handlebars pulled back to somewhere near their original shape, I was allowed back on the road.

It was not long before the gremlins struck again. Both fond parents had come to the door to wish me god speed on my journey into the unknown! I waved back and lowered my goggles into position. Feeling on top of the world, I was more forceful than prudent with the kick starter, and with a sickening crash the complete gearbox was shorn from its two retaining studs, to decant itself into the road! Repairs of this nature were not easily accomplished in those days. After a lot of persuasion on my part, the local cycle dealer, a kindly soul, and one of the old school who even **made** bicycles in his workshop, accepted the errant gearbox and fitted new oversize studs to it.

By this time I had been accepted as an apprentice at Brighton locomotive works, and was now in receipt of the princely sum of 9/8d per week! The New Hudson's days were numbered. A friend of the family decided that he now did not require a 494 cc Triumph N de Luxe, on which he had only ridden for 1200 miles. Father acquired this for a reasonable figure, and at last I was able to enjoy reliable, trouble-free motoring. The New Hudson was disposed of for a few pounds, the family being jubilant at its departure. I only wish I had it now; it would be worth a fortune!

I became reasonably proficient on the Triumph and under favourable conditions I once coaxed it up to 55 mph. It was not to be however, and after I had been riding for just over a year, I had a serious mix-up with a bull-nosed Morris Oxford at a cross roads only a few yards from home. After lying by the roadside for what seemed an eternity, I was despatched to hospital in the local garage's half ton pick-up van, my broken leg sticking out of the rear door on a plank which someone had acquired from the local builders. Needless to say this brought my motorcycling career to an abrupt and inglorious end.

In those days a broken leg meant a stay in hospital of anything up to 3 months, and I managed to get discharged in time for the bonfire night celebrations. It was early in the New Year before I was passed fit for service at the works however, and motorcycling was now a dirty word in the household.

I secretly yearned to be back in the saddle, and the urge grew stronger with the passage of time. Just down the road from the works was a corner shop dabbling in motorbikes, and during my daily wanderings in the lunch hour it was not long before I became a regular visitor. A 1925 147 cc Francis Barnett 2-stroke, with a 2-speed gear box and belt drive, offered at £2, took my eye. I had managed to save enough by now to acquire a steed in this price range. No one could possibly object to such a machine; its top speed couldn't be much more than 35 mph, and it was light enough to carry. So, the two pound notes no longer burnt a hole in my pocket, and on leaving work at mid-day one Saturday I was soon astride the F.B, and setting a course for home. I had to pretend that it was really for a friend who wanted it to go to work on, and that I was going to do it up for him!

I can't say I ever did much on this machine. There was nearly always some trouble or other, not to mention the eternal belt slip and breakage. It was not long before the ruse was discovered. I looked ridiculous on it as my knees came out under the handlebars. The family noticed it too and said so, in no uncertain terms. I was told to get rid of it and obtain something more suitable; this was just what I had been waiting for. The F.B. had served its purpose. I visited the same emporium again, and at last found a 1926 250 cc side-valve Model R Matchless, which was offered for £5. The proprietor agreed to relieve me of the F.B. and allowed me my original £2. I rode it back the next Saturday and went home on the Matchless. This latter served me well. I repositioned the gear lever of the Sturmey Archer box from just under the saddle nose to a horizontal position for foot change, as was a popular custom at that time. Then of course, you had to be careful in selecting second gear as there was no 'stop'.

I even went to London on the thing one Sunday, in the company of my two colleagues. When the second one of the pair exchanged his 250 cc round tank BSA for a 250 cc ohv Ariel, I could no longer keep up with them. The days of the Matchless then were numbered!

About this time a certain T.W. Fassett, who had ridden an Ariel in the Manx Grand Prix, opened a motor cycle business in the town where I lived. I went along and found a nice 250 cc Rudge, with an ohv JAP engine, of 1930 vintage. The Matchless was left behind and at last I was astride a mount with an ohv engine, with the added bonus of the superb Rudge coupled brakes, the front one no less than 8 inches in diameter. The machine's drawback, which I was unaware of for some time, was its weight. It was really a 350 cc bike fitted with a 250 cc engine. I was no dwarf or lightweight. Even so, I managed to coax nearly 70 mph out of it. As mentioned earlier, I had joined the local motorcycle club with it and it was not long before I was going to grass track meetings and trials sections with them - as a spectator of course.

I thoroughly enjoyed these outings, and when the Club staged its members only Pillion Trial in the Autumn of 1931, I entered and persuaded a fellow apprentice at the works to be my pillion passenger. We got on very well and to my surprise and delight, I won the Premier Award. A silver cup for me and a box of cigarettes for Tom. This early success decided me to launch my competition career and I entered several much more important trials. Lack of experience, and insufficient power in the motor told, however, and no more awards came my way. At one section I came to a standstill in the mud. A steward came up to give me a hand. 'Open her up' he exclaimed, 'It's the only way you'll get up'. 'Can't do it chum' I exclaimed. 'Why not' asked the steward. 'She's flat out already' I replied, so our combined efforts had to assist the poor little motor to the top!

I was determined to pursue my trials urge and, if possible, to try some grass track racing. At the 1931 Motor Cycle Show I was very impressed with the newly introduced Excelsior B14 model, fitted with a 498 cc racing JAP engine and reputed to being capable of 100 mph, with tuning. I knew from reading the Brooklands reports in *The Motor Cycle* that these machines had virtually monopolised the Outer Circuit events, and I asked Tom Fassett if he could get one for me. He said he could, but I would do

My first ohv mount, 1930
246 cc Rudge Whitworth JAP ⇨

⇦ First taste of success. The Rudge
wins the Premier Award in the Brighton &
District MCC's Pillion Trial, Autumn 1931

My first Ariel. A 1932 499 cc ⇨
4 valve Red Hunter bought in
the Spring of 1932

much better with the also newly introduced 500 cc Ariel Red Hunter. The latter would be much better suited to mud plugging, with its upswept exhaust system and higher ground clearance, and as it was claimed to be capable of 90 mph, Tom's salesmanship prevailed. He was, after all, the local Ariel agent, and so on the day preceding Good Friday 1932 I left the Rudge with him, and rode out on the Ariel. The very first ride on that Thursday evening, on my first brand new machine, was an unforgettable experience. The Red Hunter was a very striking machine, with its chromium plated tank having two small red panels emblazoned with the legend Ariel, and a top red panel which served as an instrument housing, encompassing the 100 mph speedometer and the oil pressure gauge. The highly polished upswept exhaust pipes, terminating in circular section *Carbjector* silencers, and chromium wheel rims with red centres completed the picture; I was indeed proud to be astride such a machine.

I decided on the seven mile ride into Brighton to go and show my new steed to the club secretary. All went well on the level road along the coast, but he lived at the top of the hill flanking the northern end of Preston Park. This caused me to use a little more throttle in second (it had a 3-speed gearbox only), and to my surprise and dismay the engine tightened up, in this, its first ten miles. I had not experienced anything of this nature before, but remembered reading in *The Motor Cycle* about disengaging the clutch in such circumstances. I was extremely quick in the application of this technique, and came to an inglorious halt at the roadside.

The fumes from the frying cylinder-black paint on the fins smelt anything but pleasant, and I just sat there and smoked a cigarette whilst the engine cooled down. The cigarette finished, I was most relieved to discover that the kickstarter caused the engine to rotate. I had very gingerly pressed down on it with some trepidation, but all was well and the engine restarted without further ado. I duly found the secretary and after he had admired my new mount, I returned home without further bother.

Several times during my ownership of this machine it locked up solid on me, despite relieving the offending high spots on the slipper-type piston. Five bolts secured the cylinder head to the barrel, and I subsequently found that the best policy was to ignore the centre bolt in the front, between the exhaust ports, and tighten the other four in the orthodox manner. The fifth one was then replaced and just lightly nipped up to block the hole. No further trouble was experienced with seizures after this. I always thought that the uneven pull of five bolts caused barrel distortion, with the subsequent risk of piston seizure.

I always thought this particular type of Red Hunter was based on the old Rudge racers, as it had a four valve pent roof head with parallel valves, and an 'oversquare' engine of 86.5 x 85 mm bore and stroke, giving a capacity of 499 cc. The makers offered it for only the one year, 1932. Subsequent Hunters used a two-valve head, with the option of one or two exhaust ports.

Chapter Two

TT Week in the Isle of Man

Upon joining the local Brighton & District Motorcycle Club in the summer of 1931, it was not long before I made the acquaintance of Bill Bottin, who lived at Shoreham-by-Sea, only about a mile from me. Bill had a 346 cc ohv Levis in trials trim, and it was his intention to take part in as many of these events as he could. We went to several together during the autumn and winter of '31 and '32, and discussed the possibility of going over to the Isle of Man, to see the TT, the dream of most motorcyclists of those days. Bill managed to get his holiday week to coincide with TT week and as I had now my new 500 cc Ariel, I asked at the works for the same week, and was granted permission.

For some time before the great day we prepared the machines. Quite an elaborate carrier for the machines, similar to that standard on a lot of present day models, but without the top-box was evolved and fixed to the rear of the Levis. As we intended to camp on any suitable site we could find, the tent was entrusted to this carrier. Ancillary gear was stowed in two ex-army rucksacks, and attached, pannier-fashion, one on each side of the Ariel.

We had arranged to start early on the Sunday morning and the great day dawned bright and sunny. We bade our respective families goodbye and headed into the unknown - destination the ticket office of the Isle of Man Steam Packet Company, on the pier at Liverpool.

Somewhere north of Oxford I was leading and, looking round saw no sign of Bill, so I eased off on the twist grip and took it steady for a couple of miles. Again I turned around and still drew a blank, so decided to call a halt to await his arrival. It was just as well. No sooner had the Ariel settled on its stand than the pungent smell of hot rubber assailed my nostrils, and an ominous coil of smoke rose steadily upwards from the offside pannier! The unsprung rear wheel had given the panniers a rough time of it, and they had gradually settled down to rest on the tops of the upswept silencers, which arrested their further downward progress. Further examination revealed that the offside pannier had deposited its base in a black, sticky, stinking mess all over the pristine chrome of the *Carbjector* silencer. The contents of this pannier had been wrapped in my brand new rubber ground sheet, and this now had a sizeable hole burnt in it, glowing red at the edges! My gloved hand dealt with the smouldering edges and I laid the contents out to cool down. As the groundsheet had been folded, I undid it and laid it out on the bank. Instead of one hole, I now had upwards of a dozen, and as I stood surveying its now well ventilated appearance, Bill arrived and dryly observed, 'I'm glad my gear was in the other side pannier', which luckily had not quite reached the other silencer!

Between us we refixed the errant panniers, repacked the gear and resumed our northward journey. No further untoward incidents impeded our progress, and after negotiating the newly opened Mersey tunnel, we duly fetched up on the steamer quay, somewhere around 8.00 pm on a lovely summer evening. Neither of us had ever experienced a ride of this length before and we both felt very tired, and very scruffy. We espied a very convenient bench and after shedding waders, competition coats, goggles, gloves and all the other impedimenta that motorcyclists of the day arrayed themselves in, we stretched out our weary limbs and set about the remains of the provisions we had left, plus the remains of the flask of tea – by now rather unpalateable, and decidedly lukewarm!

Bill Bottin (left) and the Author, equipped for the trip to the Isle of Man in June 1932

After a nice rest we found the *Ben-my-Chree*, and were advised of the 'modus operandi' by a crew member we were fortunate enough to encounter on the quay side. Thanks to the assistance of this gallant matelot, it was not long before the bikes and ourselves were safely aboard, having first, of course, been subject to the attention of the RAC man with his portable pump. After this worthy had done his duty, our bikes were emblazoned with the legend 'Tank Empty' in large white letters on a red background, the sticky backs of which were rendered operative by rapid contact with the large, wet, red tongue of the RAC guide.

The bikes were duly stowed amidships along with the others, and having several hours before sailing time, we explored the vessel. After a very welcome wash in the gents we found the refreshment bar, where we abated our hunger and slaked the prodigious thirst we had developed. Around midnight the boat departed, and we settled down in a cosy corner to try and get some sleep.

I don't think either of us slept much. Luckily the crossing was quite a smooth one, but we felt rather cold, in spite of having re-donned our motorcycle coats and gloves. Never having had much ambition to leave my native shores, this was the longest sea voyage I had ever undertaken, and as events turned out, ever did make! As the dawn broke we strolled up on deck, and as light improved we could see the Snaefell masif of the Island, standing out clearly from the low ground of the sea shore, the latter being shrouded in mist. It was an unforgettable sight, approaching the Island on a perfect sunny, summer morning. After what seemed an eternity the boat ground to a halt alongside the quay.

Before the boat had even come to rest, a group of burly dockers had leapt aboard, reminiscent of the pirates of days gone by boarding a prize merchantman; 'Want yer bike off guvnor?' one bawled at me, an obvious prospective client clad in motorcycle coat. 'Er, Yes' I replied, somewhat shaken by the rapidity of events. 'Where it is mate?' came from a tall lithe fellow, who had leapt on to the saddle of the outside machine, and stood poised there awaiting my directions. 'The one with the red and chrome tank with pannier bags on, way over to your right' I shouted at him. Without further ado, he leapt on to the saddle of each intervening bike in turn to reach my Ariel. He was already joined by a colleague with a similar gait before he had reached my bike, then between them, they lifted it up bodily and marched back over the other bikes with it in their arms! I thanked my lucky stars that mine was the first one selected, and that it was not on the outside of the stack, to be trampled over by the dockers. Bill had also enlisted the aid of a pair of toughs, and we were the first two off the boat. The tide was out, and the quayside towered above us so, having re-imbursed our new-found helpers, we had to manhandle the bikes up the steps to the quay's road.

Once on the quay, the sight of the waiting RAC guide with his portable pump, beckoning us unto him was most welcome, and each bike received a 'shot', sufficient to 'Get you to a garage on the Island' as our benefactor informed us.

The Island appeared deserted; small wonder, as it was only around 6 am, so we started our bikes and made our way inland over empty roads. We soon realized that we were actually on the famous

Bill Bottin clings to the tent for support. Our camp site at St. Johns

The Author also needs the tent's support. The farm buildings can be seen in the background

course, as we saw the signs for the various corners. It was as if we had landed on another planet, no idea where we were, and no one around to ask. At last we found a milkman on his morning round, complete with pony and milk float. We immediately hove to, and I asked our saviour if he knew of any likely camping sites, where we could pitch camp for race week. 'Knows the very place for ee' he replied. 'Gaw darn this yere road till yer gits ter Ballacraine carner' he advised. 'Dawn't goo rand carner, but straaight on, soign-pasted St. Jawhns. As yere craws stream, they be a varm on ya rite, ya'll zee rowd up t'it. Varmer they'rll make thee walcome'. After pausing a few minutes to translate it, I felt fairly confident of my ability to locate this desirable Utopia, thanked him kindly and hoped our meagre petrol supply from the RAC would enable us to motor there, without recourse to physical effort.

Ballacraine seemed a long way off. I suppose that at the leisurely gait at which we were proceeding, looking for the 'St. Jawhns' signpost, it seemed further than it really was, but at last I saw the two halves of the big red board with Bllr. Craine on it, and also the St. Johns signpost. The farm proved easy to find, not very far along and surprise! we saw a garage with a real 'Bowser' petrol pump attached, just past the farm road.

The 'Varmer' turned out to be a very friendly specimen, and directed us to a site on rising ground overlooking a lovely little brook, the waters of which he assured us were pure and suitable for washing and drinking. Farm produce, butter, eggs, milk, home cured bacon etc., were available at his back door, and we unpacked in the sunshine, feeling on top of the world!

The tent was soon erected, and the lovely fresh bacon and eggs that Bill cooked were very much appreciated, and rapidly disposed of. Then the awful truth dawned on us. It was Monday, Junior TT day, and the race started at 10 am. No time to wash up! Everything was bundled haywire into the tent and the flap secured. We leapt aboard the bikes and made back towards Ballacraine. The course road was now closed, and a convenient field had its gate open and was being used as an impromptu bike park.

15

We left our bikes, and walked the rest of the way to the corner, securing a vantage point just in time. Within minutes a marshall blew his whistle and we peered up the road. Then I caught sight of a leather-clad figure approaching at speed, the number 'one' prominently attached to his front forks, but surprisingly, I heard no sound until he closed the throttle, when a roar reminiscent of calico being torn smote our ears! Then he laid the model over and opened the taps. It was Otto Steinfellner, from Austria, on a 349 cc Rudge, and it sounded beautiful as it vanished rapidly into the distance.

Of all the racing bikes I have heard in my life since then, none had such a profound effect on my mind as the sound and sight of that four valve TT Rudge, my first sight and sound of a TT bike in full cry!

The marshal's whistle sounded every time a rider was sighted, sometimes twice in rapid succession, meaning that two were coming together, an added thrill. We stayed at the corner for the duration of the race, and thoroughly enjoyed our first Junior TT. All the bikes sounded the same as that very first Rudge, almost inaudible until they shut off. Then came the calico tearing and the bellow as they opened up on leaving the corner; it was superb! Remember, this was before the day of the megaphone exhaust, pioneered by Rudges, a few years after this. This day all the models had long, open pipes reaching to the rear spindle.

The racing over, we collected our bikes and made back to the tent. We thought it prudent to visit the local garage first, however, and were relieved to receive two gallons of No 1 petrol apiece, via the 'Bowser' we had located earlier that morning. The chores were soon disposed of. Then we had another good meal off the local produce, left everything shipshape and Bristol fashion, having decided to visit the Island's capital, Douglas.

The first thing to claim our attention was a visit to Athol Street to acquire the necessary Manx Road Fund License. Then we explored the town. The late Junior TT competitors seemed to be everywhere. Bikes with open exhausts, still displaying their racing numbers, and devoid of registration plates, were being ridden with gay abandon, and no one seemed to take any exception to them, in fact just the reverse.

We were now able to ascertain that Stanley Woods had brought his 348 cc Norton home to win at 77.16 mph. Second was Wal Handley at 76.36 mph on a 349 cc Rudge, and third H.G. Tyrell Smith on another 349 cc Rudge at 74.02 mph.

We were very interested in the antiquated horse trams, and enjoyed a leisurely half hour sampling the joys they provided. Passengers joined and departed as they pleased, often not bothering to stop the tram but just stepping on or off during its normal progress!

It had been a perfect day weather-wise, racing, and holiday wise, and we returned to camp, tired, but well pleased with our first day.

The next day was taken up with, first of all, a run round the course, starting and finishing at Ballacraine. After that, sight seeing; St. John's, Peel, on to Ramsey, the Laxey Wheel and back over Snaefell.

For the Lightweight Race on the Wednesday, we decided to get up on the mountain section, but reached only Hillberry before the road was closed to wheeled traffic. We were directed into a field once more, left the bikes, and then proceeded up the course to Brandish corner, where we were finally halted by the marshal in charge. We had no option but to sit down on the bank and watch the race from there.

From here you could see up the hill to Creg-ny-baa, and downhill to Hillberry, and also see the lads tearing down from Keppel gate to the Craig hotel, although they were only specks in the distance on this stretch. The weather had deteriorated slightly, and it ultimately became rather misty. Not such an enjoyable day as the Monday, we voted. Back in Douglas we learned that Leo Davenport on a 246 cc New Imperial had won at 70.48 mph, Graham Walker was second on a 249 cc Rudge at 70.07 mph and Wal Handley was third on a 249 cc Rudge at 69.86 mph.

More sight-seeing followed on Thursday and another run round the course for good measure. We were very intrigued to see the lines left on the road by the tyres, at bends and corners. It was as if someone had taken a giant pencil and traced lines through the bend. All these lines were in a very narrow band, little more than a foot wide, denoting that the riders all used the same piece of road.

For the Senior Race on the Friday we decided to motor up to Creg-ny-baa and park the bikes on the road which joined the course at this point. This would allow us to use the bikes to visit different vantage points during the race, on roads not closed to the public. There was very much more traffic about; several boatloads of enthusiasts with their bikes had come over from the mainland just for the Senior. We watched the first lap from Creg-ny-baa. Then we collected our bikes and made a long detour to come out near Signpost corner. After a spell here we again shifted and finished in the Grandstand area. I don't think we gained much by this gadding about. In fact we missed quite a bit of the race whilst motoring around the hinterland. For my part, I had enjoyed the Junior most of all at Ballacraine.

Thanks to our run round the course of the previous day and our haste to beat the road closure of the morning, inspection now revealed that the Ariel had just about enough petrol on board to flood the carburettor. Bill's Levis had not been so thirsty but the problem was how to transfer the fuel from Levis to Ariel. The only thing we had remotely suitable was the canvas carrying case of my *No 2 Brownie* camera. We must have looked a pair of Charlies holding this case under Bill's petrol tap (with pipe attached) slowly filling this case, whilst petrol dripped out all around it, as it proved anything but petrol proof!

After wasting a half hour or so on these antics, we decided there should now be enough to enable me to reach a more orthodox means of replenishment, so we set course for Douglas. We soon found a filling station and slaked the Ariel's thirst. 'Don't think I'll bother to buy anymore' said Bill, rocking the Levis from side to side whilst he scanned the agitating fuel content through the filler cap's neck. 'We're off home in the morning, and I'll only have to give it all to the RAC on the pier.' 'Please yourself' I said, 'But I must have some, RAC notwithstanding'.

We went back to Douglas for a last look at the holiday resort. It had been another gorgeous day weather-wise, and Stanley Woods had again led, to complete his double at 79.38 mph on a 490 cc Norton. The incomparable Jimmy Guthrie took second place at 78.47 mph and 'Tiger' Jimmy Simpson finished third at 78.38 mph, making another Norton hat trick. Jimmy Simpson became the first man to lap the Island at over 80 mph, a wonderful feat we thought, after our own attempts over the same circuit.

We did not stay very late in Douglas that evening. We had to be up bright and early next day to pack up and board the morning boat for Liverpool. We woke up in good time, breakfasted on the local produce for the last time, then cleaned up the camp site, burying all our rubbish. With a heavy heart we dismantled and stowed the tent and packed up the bits and pieces in the panniers, which by this time had been re-positioned on the Ariel. It had been a truly wonderful week's holiday, with no rain at all. The misty Wednesday was the only doubtful day. We made our way to the arm to take leave of our wonderful host 'The Varmer'. The latter wished us a pleasant journey home and would not dream of accepting any money for our stay on his land. That we had enjoyed our stay with him, he declared, was sufficient reimbursement for him.

We were loath to depart, but the time of sailing crept ever nearer, so we reluctantly bade our final farewells and headed for Douglas.

We hadn't reached Crosby when I heard an SOS on the Levis's horn, and glanced round just in time to see Bill coasting to a stand by the grass verge. I stopped and Bill paddled the recalcitrant Levis alongside. 'What's up?' I queried. 'Bloody thing's run out of petrol' he gasped. This was serious. There was none too much time as it was, and I feverishly started searching for something to rectify matters, when I suddenly remembered old faithful, the camera case! Once more it was filled with petrol, this time from the Ariel's tap, and with much spilling and cursing the Levis was replenished. Tools were hastily restowed, coats buttoned up and we were away once more.

We arrived breathless on the quay, to find the RAC man could not get any petrol out of Bill's tank, much to the latter's delight! There was precious little to be obtained from the Ariel either, after the little episode up the road! Our willing friends, the dockers, hove in sight, but we did not require their services this time. The tide was up, so the boat was almost level with the quay, and we were able to wheel our own steeds on board. The crew stowed them amidships again and a rope was secured around them. Within a few minutes there was a sharp blast on the ship's siren and the propellers began to churn up the mud in the harbour. We had only just made it! We stood on deck and saluted the fading Mona's Isle. It had been the most wonderful holiday we ever had.

Chapter Three
The Brooklands Bug Bites

I did not wish immediately to cover my nice, new, shiny motorbicycle with the mud of trials sections, so I kept it to the main road and took the opportunity of making the acquaintance of Brooklands Motor Course, Weybridge, Surrey, as it was officially styled, for their first meeting in 1932.

I was most impressed. The deep note emitted from those Brooklands 'silencers' was music to my ears. I thought they were more like amplifiers than silencers. I had never previously seen machinery moving at such a prodigious rate. Immediately I coveted a very smart, all copper-plated machine, described in the programme as a 498 cc Bickell JAP. In later years I ascertained that this mile eater was the brain-child of one Joe Bickell who, with his brother Ben, ran a motorcycle business in Archway Road, Highgate, London N. In those days the AA patrols were equipped with Chater-Lea side-valve motorcycles, attached to closed box-type sidecars, loaded with all sorts of equipment. The story goes that one of the said outfits got bent about in some kind of fracas, and was duly deposited at the Archway Road premises for attention. The sidecar was apparently fit for further service, but the powers that be decided against similar treatment for the motorcycle. More for a joke than anything else, Joe decided to turn it into a Brooklands racer, and after 'cutting the frame about a bit', to quote his own words, he installed a very potent 498 cc JAP racing engine, over which he had waved his magic wand. The entire metal structure, excepting the engine, was then copper plated, and the riding entrusted to brother Ben. The result was a unique and very attractive ensemble, and to see this machine passing the fork grandstand, my vantage point that day, at about 112 mph was a sight I shall never forget. Ben had gained his 'Gold Star' with it the previous year.

I must admit I was quite appalled by the track's surface. I had always imagined a beautiful, dead smooth, saucer of concrete on which it was a joy to go fast. Instead I found quite small 'bays', the joints between the individual sections being just the reverse of precision workmanship, and in places showing gaping holes in their surface. All the more remarkable I realised, the feat of C.W.G. (Bill) Lacey who, in 1928 had covered no less than 103 miles in one hour on this wretched surface, riding his 498 cc Grindlay-Peerless JAP. What a hammering his poor body must have endured on that meteoric ride. The track was nicknamed 'The Bumpy Bowl' I later ascertained.

The severity of the hairpin bend at The Fork also surprised me. It needed superb judgement to negotiate that right hander in the Mountain Circuit I concluded, as it was approached downhill, and at speeds close to three figures by the fastest riders. It was possible to go straight on up the other track however, if one was unable to reduce to a suitable gait for safe navigation, a facility I found most welcome in later years. I had recourse to proceed up that slip road for a considerable distance, in my last year at the track, when my brakes appeared to do nothing at all to impede my progress towards impending disaster.

I made several more trips to Weybridge during the year, and found them most enjoyable. The absence of any large number of spectators amazed me. At times I had the various public enclosures to myself, and sometimes it seemed there was more competitors than spectators!

Ben Bickell on his 498 cc Bickell JAP, taken on 15th August 1931 *(Motor Cycle)*

My first 'racer'. The four valve 499 cc Ariel in grass track trim during 1933

C.W.G. Lacey raised the World's 1 hour record with this 497 cc Grindlay Peerless JAP, covering 103 miles 532 yards on 1st August 1928. He thus became the first man to cover 100 miles in the hour on a British track. His machines were always spotless, hence his nickname, Nickel Plate Lacey *(Motor Cycle)*

Worried about the development of the multi cylinder machine abroad, whilst British manufacturers concentrated on the well tried 'one lunger', *The Motor Cycle* offered a cup for the first British multi cylinder 500 cc machine to cover 100 miles in the hour.

Ariel motors, early in the 1930's, had introduced the Square Four. This was a 500 cc four cylinder model with two crankshafts geared together, the cylinder bores having a square formation, one in each corner. A chain-driven overhead camshaft looked after the valve operation, and the machine had a very lively performance, with particularly rapid acceleration.

Brooklands ace Ben Bickell decided that here was the very machine with which to annexe this award, so brother Joe immediately set about preparing one for the task. The usual Brooklands features were installed, such as a racing saddle over the wheel, dropped handlebars, Outer Circuit type front wheel, Brooklands silencers, and last, but by no means least, a supercharger. Ariel motors also co-operated and supplied a huge petrol tank, to cope with the prodigious thirst of the blown motor. My photograph shows it in November 1933.

Each time Ben had a crack at the record, he was dogged by misfortune. The cylinder head gasket was a regular culprit. The cylinder base flange also had a tendency to part from the cylinder block. Ernie Smith at the Selly Oak factory tried his hardest to get a special block made up with a more robust flange, but the designer, Edward Turner, declined, insisting that everything must be standard. Conveniently, he ignored the supercharger!

Attempts continued throughout 1934, always with the same result. The Ariel would lap consistently at around 110 mph. Once the rear tyre shed all of its tread, and several times the magneto packed up. At

20

Ben Bickell's supercharged 500 cc Ariel 4 with which he hoped to win the *Motor Cycle* Trophy for the first British 500 cc multi to cover 100 miles in the hour. Photo taken on 23rd November 1933

Right-hand side of the power plant of the supercharged Ariel 4

S. (Ginger) Wood covered 102 miles 475 yards in 1 hour on 1st August 1934 to win the *Motor Cycle* Cup for the first British multi-cylinder 500 cc to cover 100 miles in the hour. He rode this 492 cc New Imperial twin *(Motor Cycle)*

this time the 500 cc lap record stood to the credit of W.J.C. Hewitt, 498 cc Excelsior JAP, at a speed of 115.29 mph established on 23rd July 1932.

But other eyes were also on the coveted award. New Imperial Motors had mounted two of their racing 250 cc 'pots' on a common crankcase, and this machine had proved itself to have the speed, over in the Isle of Man. The handling, however, was quite another matter. As both are required in the Isle of Man, it did not exactly show the Nortons the way round. But 100 miles in the hour on Brooklands might be more within its capabilities, providing its navigator was endowed with a pair of strong wrists, the only deterrent to its meandering tendencies. S. 'Ginger' Wood was a rider of indomitable courage, and having also the requisite wrists of steel, he was selected for this unenviable assignment.

So it was on 1st August 1934 that the New Imperial team arrived at Brooklands, unloaded one of the 500 cc TT twins and set about the acquisition of this trophy. The day was cool, with low lying cloud and a high wind. Everything seemed to indicate that rain was imminent. However, by 5.30 pm the wind had dropped, and Ginger put in a couple of preliminary laps to ascertain if conditions were suitable.

The answer was in the affirmative, and Ginger rode it up to the line. The regulations required a push start. George Reynolds, the timekeeper, dropped his flag and Pa Archer, father of Les, acted as pusher off. First time round Ginger appeared very happy, and was sitting back over the rear wheel, lying absolutely flat over the tank. The standing lap had been reeled off at 97.27 mph. Next time round it had risen to 106.88 mph and the next one still further to 107.8 mph.

Matt Wright, O.C. engine, was now smiling, and gave Ginger the signal to ease up a trifle. So he settled down to a steady 105 to 106 mph, seldom varying by more than a mile an hour. By the end of the tenth lap he had averaged 105.29 mph.

L.J. Archer on a New Imperial with sidecar outside his shed at Brooklands in 1929 *(L.J. Archer)*

25th August 1934. Eric Fernihough, 173 cc Excelsior JAP, finds time to grin at C.K. Mortimer, 246 cc New Imperial (23), as he wins the 'Hutchinson Hundred' at 82.18 mph. The New Imp has a slow puncture in the rear tyre *(Motor Cycle)*

On his eighteenth lap Ginger was signalled to come in for fuel next time round. He was now 1 minute 30 seconds in front of his schedule. When he had settled down once more, he had 49 seconds in hand. His pit stop, including deceleration and acceleration, had cost 51 seconds. He was now given the order to ease up still further, and he settled down to lap between 100 and 102 mph.

So much had he in hand that by his thirty fifth lap, with only a little more than two to go, he slowed even more, to just under the 100 mark. Even so he had averaged 102.27 mph in one hour and 6 seconds! So the New Imperial concern were the victors in this most gruelling contest, in which all three other contestants had been dogged by misfortune. The machine used differed but little from the TT machine. The fuel used was alcohol and the compression ratio had been increased to suit. Bronze single port heads were used. Each had its own downdraught carburettor, inclined at thirteen degrees.

What of those less fortunate? Everyone had great sympathy for Ben Bickell and his supercharged Ariel four. In several attempts Ben had covered twice the required distance at well over 103 mph, but always some trouble or other would put him out of the running.

Triumphs also had just developed a supercharged twin which had begun to lap at over 105 mph. C.T. Atkins had also made several attempts in 1932 and 33 on a Douglas.

Although the cup had been won, the contestants didn't relax. On 25th August they were both entered in the Hutchinson Hundred at Brooklands. The New Imperial was ridden this time by Jock Forbes as Ginger had been one of those involved in the notorious crash at the Ulster Grand Prix. Les Archer was another so involved, and he too was a non-starter. The New Imp received 27 seconds start on the Ariel, which was on the scratch mark. The latter made a very inspiring getaway. Pushed off, it spluttered once or twice, moved forward slowly for a yard or two with a polite purr, and then seemed suddenly to gather itself together and swoop away, letting out a tearing snarl that had to be heard to be believed. Just 17 minutes 13 seconds had elapsed since the limit man, Eric Fernihough, had been

Monty Saunders on the streamlined 248 cc Excelsior JAP finished third in the 3 lap handicap on 26th August 1933 with laps at 88.15, 102.27 and 102.48 mph. He also covered 5 miles at 102.36 mph
(K.R. Blake)

despatched, and he had completed about 8 laps in this time. He proved the winner at 82.18 mph.

Although Jock Forbes had not ridden it until that morning, the New Imp proceeded to lap at 106 to 107 mph, and he was delighted with the handling of it. After 14 laps, however, the fork spring broke in two places and gave Jock some anxious moments on the Byfleet Banking until he could arrest its hectic progress.

In the meantime, Ben was snarling round at 109 mph., but one lap after the demise of the New Imperial, as if to be in sympathy with it, the snarl suddenly changed to an abrupt *Brrp*, followed by a sudden deathly silence as the Ariel passed the Vickers sheds. It had made the fastest lap in the race at 109.70 mph whilst the New Imp's best had been 106.65 mph. W.C. Marshall, on a rapid Excelsior JAP had put in a lap at 104.63 mph before it stripped a head bolt, and thus terminated his lappery for the day.

Eric's four year old Excelsior raised the 175 cc lap record, which he held already, by 1 mph to 85.83 mph.

Having had the 200 guinea Mellano Trophy, the prize for winning the 'Hutchy', snatched from their grasp by a 175 cc 'baby', New Imperial Motors decided that in future they would field machinery that would make the others sit up and take notice. If it could last the distance, there was no doubt in the Boardroom that the trophy would repose there in the very near future.

So again they entered the 500 cc twin in the 'Hutchy', held on 28th September 1935. To set seal on this project, and made doubly sure of success, Matt Wright and the boffins at the factory had clapped a supercharger on, virtually overnight, which entailed lengthening the frame. The machine duly arrived at the track on the morning of the race in the works van, and Ginger was soon out on it. It then became apparent that the blower and lengthened frame had done nothing to improve the handling qualities; in fact they were even worse than before!

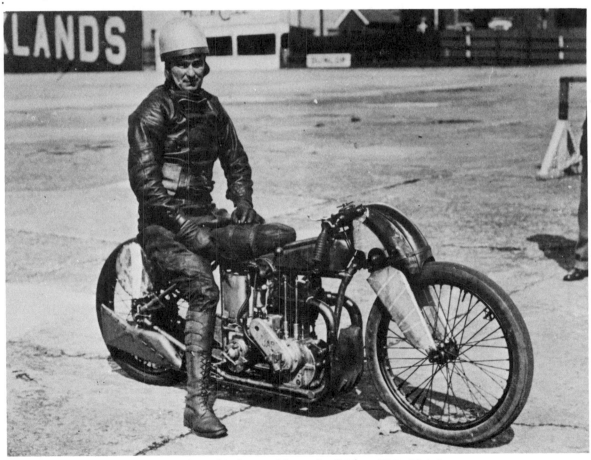

Monty could lap at about 96 mph in this form without the fairing (K.R. Blake)

I was helping at the pits in this event, and had a grandstand view of it from the fork. Ginger, of course, was scratch, and the limit man had completed eight laps, and most of the others at least one, before the New Imperial was signalled away.

The first time it came round past the fork, it was obvious that we were in for some excitement, and we all concentrated our attention on it. It came past the fork in one long slide, almost broadside, more like a dirt track bike than a Brooklands one. After a few laps of this we all began to speculate as to just how long Ginger would survive. We were interrupted by the loud speaker blaring out, 'On his last lap Ginger Wood raised the 500 cc lap record to 115.82 mph'. This was his third lap. We were all agog at this, but the stewards did not share our enthusiasm. They had held a hurried consultation, and decided that his progress was highly dangerous. For the safety of the other riders, not to mention his own, they decided to disqualify him.

A marshal took up position with a huge board displaying Ginger's number in one hand, and the ominous black flag in the other. We all waited. Surely he should have been here by now? Sure enough, the slower men had completed another lap, but there was still no sign of our hero. The loadspeaker blared again. 'If anyone knows the whereabouts of Ginger Wood, would they please communicate with the stewards.'

Ginger himself, so I was told, heard this and walked into the steward's abode, to the surprise of the occupants. The dirt track performance was more than the rear tyre was prepared to endure, and it signified so by parting company with the rim. This in turn caused the New Imp, by now nicknamed 'The Camel', to dispatch Ginger into the dust out Byfleet way, whilst it continued riderless on its course to destruction. Miraculously, the rider was only slightly hurt, and he made his way back to the start, to arrive in time to answer the summons to the stewards.

Earlier in the same year, during the 100 miles Brooklands Grand Prix, I had great admiration for this same rider, again mounted on 'The Camel', sans supercharger, when he led the field in the Senior Race. As he swept through the artificial bends formed by the oil drums, he would release the tension of the handlebar controlled steering damper, and reset it as he left, by bringing his left hand right over to the lever, adjacent to his twist grip on the right hand side. This avoided having to release his right hand from the grip, risking possible throttle closure. Ginger won this event at 76.93 mph.

Ben was also peeved at having to retire before half distance during the 1934 Hutchinson 100, so he decided to try once more, with the result that the pair of them occupied scratch position.

The crowd thoroughly enjoyed the music when the flag fell, as Ben's four emitted a snarling yowl, and Ginger's twin a high pitched crackle, as they went through the gears.

The Ariel had the advantage on acceleration, but by the time they reached the Members' Banking, the New Imp was in the lead. These two had to concede 25 minutes 17 seconds, to the limit man, R.E. Cramp, on a 249 cc Excelsior. They would obviously have to do some exceedingly fast motoring if they were to catch him in 100 miles!

Ginger was lapping at 114 mph to start with, getting faster each lap, and breaking the lap record at almost 116 mph on his third circuit. But as already related, his time was running out and he failed to complete lap five. Meanwhile, Ben's Ariel had not been firing too evenly from the start, and he decided it was hopeless, retiring after six laps.

History, therefore, repeated itself and both riders retired at almost the same time. Cramp meanwhile had failed to complete even one lap, so Noel Christmas romped home the winner, having averaged 97.46 mph on his 348 cc Velocette whilst Jock West was second on a 493 cc Triumph at 100.01 mph, the only rider to exceed the 'ton'.

The early 1930's were great days at Brooklands. I was a regular visitor, and even after I became a competitor I still enjoyed watching the events in which I was not competing. I also made the acquaintance of several very famous riders of the day. Such men as E.C.E. Baragwanath, affectionately known as 'Barry', who first raced there in 1912, the year I was born! I always remember him for his wing collar; I never saw him without one! On his 996 cc Brough Superior JAP, to which he had added a supercharger, he raised the sidecar lap record to 103.97 mph in July 1933, before he retired from racing at the end of that year. He was always about the place though, either as Scrutineer in the Paddock, or as Chief Marshal. Also in July 1933, A.L. Loweth on a **side-valve** 490 cc Norton averaged 89.9 mph in the 50 mile New Zealand Handicap, with a best lap at 93.97 mph. Even that was not the Norton's limit, as two years earlier he had lapped with it at 96 mph.

Then there was the incomparable Eric Fernihough and his remarkable 175 cc Excelsior JAP, who raised the 175 cc lap record to 84.92 mph in the autumn of '33. I happened to be present that day as it was my 21st birthday!

Another highlight in my spectating calendar occurred on 26 th August 1933. Then M.B. Saunders on a 246 Excelsior JAP raised the 250 cc lap record to no less than 102.48 mph, to gain the only 250 cc Gold Star ever awarded at the track. A special streamlined form was evolved for this attempt, the machine having been prepared by J.S. 'Wooly' Worters, a wizard Brooklands tuner. Because of the streamlining, it was nearly 18 months before the machine could be taken out for this attempt, I was told. If the wind strength exceeded about 20 mph, the machine was a non-starter, as it adversely affected the steering. Both these 175 cc and 250 cc records remained intact, never having been bettered by the time the track closed in 1939.

In the meantime I had now got over the novelty of the new machine, and had commenced competing in hill climbs, small grass track circuits etc., run by clubs near home. Not without success. The Ariel did me very well in a series of hill climbs run by the South Downs MCC, and I was the recipient of an excellent Silver Cup as their Hill Climb Champion; one that was never surpassed in size by any cup I won in subsequent years.

But the lure of Brooklands track became ever stronger, and I got my chance with *The Motor. Cycle* Clubman's day the next year. I had spent the winter months competing in various 'mud larks' officially known as trials, so I decided to take down the motor in preparation for its high speed canter. Everything was cleaned up, inspected, adjusted and renewed where required, and re-assembled with the utmost care. At last it was ready for a road test. Lying along the tank on the only suitable road in the vicinity, I recorded a good 90 mph on the speedometer. I was more than satisfied with this and the engine seemed fine. The gearchange mechanism did not appear to be too happy however, so back we went for another session in my 'works'. Several adjustments were made and a few days later, with only hours left before the great day, I carried out extensive gear changing on a different road, and the trouble seemed to have been eliminated. As a final test I decided to take the engine up to peak revs in second and then change into top. The song of that motor was exhilarating, and I was about to change when there was an awful bang, followed by much scraping and sounds of metal in torment. I declutched immediately, coasting for quite a distance. Luckily I was near home, so I pushed the rest of the way. My heart sank, as I knew there would be no tearing round Brooklands on the morrow.

Once back in the 'works' off came the head, in record time. I was appalled at the sight. Both exhaust valve heads had parted from their stems. One had stayed on top of the piston crown, worked its way round and severely lacerated both valve seats. The other had gone right through the piston to continue its devastation down below. It had bent the connecting rod and then made its exit through the bottom of the crankcase!

Needless to say I was not overjoyed to encounter these valve heads in their other than rightful positions. Realising that the Ariel certainly would not be present at Brooklands on the morrow, I dug out my trusty push bike and hied me along to my good friend Bill Bottin, the owner of a 346 cc competition Levis. Bill listened patiently as the tale of woe was unfolded. Knowing how I was looking forward to this meeting, he sportingly offered me the loan of his Levis. This offer was at once gleefully accepted (I could have kissed him!) and the Levis came home with me that night.

Although I went to the track for that meeting, I did not enjoy myself. I could not tear my thoughts away from my blown-up motor. I'm ashamed to say also that I remember nothing of what happened at that meeting.

Once back home the next thing was to arrange for the sick motor to go to hospital in Selly Oak. I procured a stout wooden box and lowered the patient inside, complete with instructions. The lid was then nailed on, resulting in a container that looked uncannily like a coffin. Along to the station I went, and surrendered it to the care of the Southern Railway Company.

Little could be salvaged from that original engine, and the invoice caused a financial depression for a considerable time afterwards. Suffice it to say that the railway company duly arrived at the family residence one day with a covered wagon, the motive power for which was supplied by an immaculate shire horse. After the necessary formalities had been completed, and forms signed in triplicate, the

In order to make his attempt on the 250 cc lap record, with his streamlined Excelsior, M.B. Saunders needed to obtain special dispensation from the British Motor-Cycle Racing Club for time to be allocated during a race meeting programme. The reply from Secretary Duncan Ferguson, as above, leaves little doubt that even Saunders was by no means sure he would succeed, let alone break the magic three figures

coffin was returned to me, and hastily relieved of its contents. The next day the Ariel was back on the road and the running-in process commenced once more.

As things settled down and I recovered from this last catastrophe, thoughts again turned to Brooklands, and the impending High Speed Trial organised by the Motor Cycling Club came to my notice. The Club hired Brooklands for the afternoon, and its members had a good day's sport on their own. This greatly appealed to me, so I joined the Club and sent in my entry. This time the Ariel reached Brooklands sound in wind and limb. The objective of the meeting was to see how many miles you could cram into one hour's navigation of the Outer Circuit. As I came under starter's orders I felt very jubilant. At last I had realised my ambition of competing at Brooklands! All went well for the first two laps. Approaching the start and finish for the third time, the now all too familiar sound of an engine crying 'enough' reached my ears, and I whipped out the clutch! I had enough 'way' on to reach the pits, and there I found that the engine had locked up solid.

The thought now uppermost in my mind was not how many miles I would be able to cram into the hour, but how the heck I was going to persuade that motor to carry me home that evening. A small posse of marshals had assembled to ascertain the cause of this latest mishap. The general concensus of opinion was that the piston had seized, and that it should free when the engine cooled down a bit. I enjoyed watching the others go by from my grandstand view at the pits, being particularly impressed by a certain W.J. Jenness from Taunton, on a 349 cc TT Replica Rudge. He came round with monotonous regularity and eventually covered 78 miles in that hour. How I envied him! His distance was the best of the day.

E.C. Baragwanath at speed on his 966 cc Brough Superior JAP on the Outer Circuit 15th August 1931
(Motor Cycle)

The one and only 'Barry' E.C.E. Baragwanath, on his supercharged Brough Superior outfit. Photo taken on 29th July 1933 *(Motor Cycle)*

The massed entry rounding the marker barrel during the Junior Grand Prix of 23rd July 1932. Some are gaining help from their feet! *(Motor Cycle)*

Rounding the fork in the Junior Grand Prix of 23rd July 1932. The two riders shown, Sid Gleave and Ted Mellors, both have 'works' status with New Imperial. Note the packed fork grandstand *(Motor Cycle)*

Rounding the fork 'en masse' in the Senior Grand Prix of 23rd July 1932. C.J. Williams (3) is riding a 494 cc Douglas and behind him there is a 'works' Rudge. F.K. Anderson (22) is riding a 498 cc Excelsior JAP and J. Piere (12) a 490 cc Norton *(Motor Cycle)*

This photograph is taken from the inside of the fork during the Senior Grand Prix of 23rd July 1932. The leading rider is C.J. Williams (3) on a 494 cc Douglas whilst (9) is probably an OK Supreme JAP *(Motor Cycle)*

Rounding Vickers Turn during the Senior Grand Prix of 23rd July 1932. The rider of the 495 cc AJS (15) is probably George Rowley and the rider of the 498 cc Excelsior JAP most likely D.J. Pirie *(Motor Cycle)*

Ernie Knott takes his 'works' Rudge through Vickers Turn during the Senior Grand Prix of 23rd July 1932 *(Motor Cycle)*

By this time the motor was stone cold, but a dig at the kickstarter revealed it was still ominously solid. Several marshals had different remedies for coaxing that recalcitrant engine back to life, but all produced the same negative result. It now became painfully obvious that something other than the piston had seized. But what? There was nothing for it but to try drastic measures. I was instructed to put the gearbox in second and three marshals would push as fast as they could. At their signal I was to release the clutch rapidly, and throw all my weight on to the saddle. This duly took place, amid much screaming of the rear tyre on the track, but I was sure that I had heard something moving amongst the machinery. The next effort produced positive results; was I pleased to hear that motor once more! It was obviously very tight and would not tick over. I decided to try and get home on it, as the oil was circulating properly and did not reveal any trouble in that direction. 'Take it steady, and with a bit of luck you should make it alright' were the comforting remarks of the Chief Marshal. I silently offered up a prayer, and set off with my heart in my mouth. The only consolation was the weather; it was a perfect evening. My prayer must have been answered, and we duly arrived home, much to my surprise.

Once more the motor was stripped but as the piston and cylinder were in good condition, the trouble was obviously in the lower half. Further dismantling revealed that the camshaft had seized solid in its bronze bush and that the bush itself had gone round in the crankcase on the way home. The camshaft had turned blue with heat so the whole timing gear and that side of the crankcase had to be renewed, as the rotating bush had not improved the aluminium housing. At least I was able to deal with this myself in my own 'works', once Selly Oak had posted me the replacement parts.

I began to wonder whether it was all worth it, as remember, I had to find every penny myself. I was still a raw tyro and no one was interested in my troubles. If it had not been for my wonderful parents, who allowed me the major part of my meagre earnings from my place of work, none of it would have been possible. I was, luckily, still living at home with them.

The latest episode caused me to abandon Brooklands aspirations, and return to trials riding, at which I was much more successful, and by now getting quite proficient.

I had taken the Ariel along to my favourite grass track, the Sydenham MCC's Mountain Mile circuit at Layhams Farm, West Wickham, Kent, and had managed to win a heat gaining a Bronze Medal. I also won a Silver Cup for second place at a Gravesend & District MCC grass track meeting, the only awards gained in grass track racing. It is worth recording that at Layhams, I first saw Harold Daniel ride, on his Norton. If he was there, the result of the race became a foregone conclusion!

By now there was a small band of enthusiasts locally, and when we went to a grass track meeting, we hired a three ton open lorry from the kindly proprietor of a local haulage firm, for whom one of our number worked as a driver. The cost was shared amongst us, the boss requiring us to meet only the ordinary running expenses. Of course, the driver, with his wife and baby, went free.

It now occurred to me that here was the answer to my Brooklands problem, and if I could conscript enough troops, with the aid of the coupon in *The Motor Cycle* to make the entry fee a viable proposition, I would be able to enter next Clubman's Day. Should the motor blow up once more, at least there would be no anxiety about getting home.

I made preliminary enquiries around the locomotive works and quite a number were keen on a visit to Brooklands. They would have to lose Saturday morning pay (not much anyway!) and the haulage contractor had very kindly co-operated by releasing his driver and lorry from their normal duties. So, when Clubman's Day, April 14th 1934 dawned, the lorry set out with some dozen or so passengers, disporting themselves around a 499 cc Red Hunter Ariel, on whatever makeshift seats they could produce. The Brooklands bug had returned, to bite even deeper during the winter months. Although I enjoyed trials riding, and to a certain extent grass track racing, my heart was really at Weybridge, notwithstanding that to date all I had been able to accomplish was 3 laps of the Outer Circuit!

I had gone over the machine very thoroughly during the preceeding weeks, and had a trial run over our test road. As far as anyone could tell, everything was in fine fettle, and I was surely due for a break.

I had entered for every event possible. In the flying kilometre trial, each entrant would receive a signed certificate of his speed, timed by the electrical apparatus, accurate to two places of decimals. The Outer Circuit scratch race and the Round the Mountain race also claimed my entries. Recent correspondence in *The Motor Cycle* had been directed at inaccurate speedometer readings at high speed.

People were not travelling anything like as rapidly as their instruments led them to believe, claimed the

At speed in between the turns during the Senior Grand Prix of 23rd July 1932. The rider is D.J. Pirie (25) on his 498 cc Excelsior JAP *(Motor Cycle)*

The massed push-start of the Junior Grand Prix held on 29th July 1933 *(Motor Cycle)*

The Junior Grand Prix of 29th July 1933. This shows the Members Banking, as viewed from the fork, with 'Chronograph Villa' on the left. A 348 cc Velocette (4) and a 348 cc AJS (8) sweep out of the turn *(Motor Cycle)*

Rounding the marker barrel in the Senior Grand Prix of 29th July 1933. The rider in white overalls (11) is on a 496 cc Cotton whilst (7) has a 498 cc Excelsior JAP *(Motor Cycle)*

The 100 miles Senior Grand Prix of 29th July 1933. Ernie Nott, sleeves rolled up, is leading and was the winner on his works Rudge. Harold Daniell, 490 cc Norton is No. 6 *(Motor Cycle)*

writer. I was convinced that MY instrument did not fall into this untruthful category, and I decided to leave it connected to give me an idea of how I was faring. I was in for a nasty shock, and about to be taught another lesson in the hard school of experience.

My very meagre experience of the Outer Circuit had enabled me to evolve a modus operandi which I thought was brilliant in its conception. Unfortunately it did not produce the shattering of the class record that I thought was inevitable! I started off and went right round the very top of the banking, then dived off it like a fighter plane in a power dive onto the timed kilometre along the Railway Straight. At the end of the dive I managed to get a good look at the speedometer. It was graduated to 100 mph, and the needle was well past that, almost round to the stop on the wrong side of the 0. I had never seen it round there before, and I felt jubilant. Along the level course of the straight it came back onto the figures again, but even at the end of the timed stretch it was still clear of 90! I remembered that the highest recorded so far was about 85 and my spirits rose. It's in the bag, so I thought! When the results were announced in the press the following week I eagerly searched for my name. Speeds were given right down to 79 mph, but I looked in vain. When my certificate came through about a week later, I found the figure incredible. It was 77.14 mph! In fairness to everybody (my friend Bill Bottin on his International 490 cc Norton the following year returned 66 mph!) I found that the prevailing wind was nearly always against you along the straight, which accounted for the low speeds. Bill tore up his certificate, but I kept mine. The kilometre trial race was memorable for one thing. For the first time in my life I received the chequered flag for completing a race at Brooklands.

The two lap Outer Circuit event was the first event after the kilometre. Two heats were required for this race; there were 35 riders in heat one and 37 in heat two. I was booked for the latter. The 350's received 26 seconds start on the 500's, the 250's 42 seconds, and the 175's 1 minute 12 seconds. The over

500's went off 4 seconds after the 500's. This handicapping favoured the 350's; they filled the first three places in heat one and first and second in heat two. The result was decided on time and A. Paul won on his Velocette at 82.45 mph, M.D. Whitworth on his 348 cc Rex Acme was second and W.J. Jenness, 349 cc Rudge, 3rd.

The three lap Mountain event for the 350's was a repeat performance, with 12 starters, all on scratch. Paul and Whitworth had a fine scrap, the former winning by a length; they were also first and second in the final placings, with H.W. Antell, the winner of heat one in third place. The winner's speed was 62.68 mph.

As there were 58 entries for the 500 cc 3 lap Mountain Race, it called for 3 heats. Heat one was won comfortably by Leonard Williams on his 596 cc Scott at 60.69 mph., P. Hewitt, on a 498 cc Excelsior JAP won the second heat at 60.17 mph and, surprise, I was second on my 499 cc Ariel!

The third heat, as might well be expected, went to Frank Williams on his Cotton, at 59.83 mph. Frank's speed over the kilo had been 84.73 mph, giving him first place, and the Excelsior had clocked 82.84 mph against my 77.14 mph.

So the final order was L.C. Williams, P. Hewitt and Frank Williams, with myself fourth. At last I had managed a day's racing at Brooklands and been second in a heat, and fourth in the final, out of 58 riders. Furthermore, both the Ariel and myself were still in one piece. I returned home feeing very pleased with myself, eventually to become the recipient of a BMCRC tankard, emblazoned with the crossed Union Jacks which formed their badge. I also received a signed certificate of my speed over the kilometre.

It seemed as if I had at last laid my Brooklands jinx by the heels. Whether the new mode of transport to meetings had any bearing on this I cannot say, but I vowed never again to ride my bike there. This way I would be sure to get home the same day!

The spectator's enclosure at the fork, prior to the start of a 3 lap Outer Circuit Handicap Race held on the 25th August 1934. The Byfleet Banking is in the background *(Motor Cycle)*

Chapter Four

The Velocettes

During my visits to grass track meetings I had been greatly impressed by the performance of the 350 cc Velocette. More riders seemed to annexe the honours on these than on any other make of machine. They also did very well at Brooklands. Our local 'star' rider, W.R. (Bill) Beamish, had recently acquired an ex-TT Velocette from A.G. Mitchell and was doing extremely well with it. It had also gained a Brooklands Gold Star at 102 mph. I decided that I would acquire one also, and started to peruse the advertisements. I had not long to wait. Ben Bickell, of Archway Road Garage fame, advertised an ex-Brooklands model, and I went along to inspect it. It was the late property of a well known Brooklands rider, H.C. Lamacraft, who had taken delivery of a new one, so was disposing of his old model. I was suitably impressed with it and acquired same. The first chance I had to use it was in the Clubman's Junior 50 miles Grand Prix at Brooklands on 28th July 1934.

The lorry and crew were duly engaged and off we went to Brooklands. Now the Velocette had one feature on it to which I was unaccustomed, a tap in the pipe leading oil from its 1 gallon oil tank to the engine. This was always left in the 'off' position when the machine was not in use. Otherwise I was told, the oil would leak down and fill up the crankcase. So far so good. I did as I was told, but anxious to get to grips with the Outer Circuit once more, I forgot to turn that tap on before starting the motor. I had completed a lap, when the awful truth dawned upon me. Was the tap off or on? I decided to investigate, so I pulled in to the side of the Railway Straight. My worst fears were realised. It was **off**! I hastily rectified matters and checked the oil flow. This seemed to be in order and as the motor seemed lively enough, practice was resumed.

Upon the race getting under way everything seemed fine, and I was congratulating myself on remembering that tap and suspending operations until the lubricant had been restored. Towards the end of the third lap, my ears were once more assailed by that 'ee, 'ee, 'ee of the rear tyre doing its best to continue its rotation against impossible odds. In a flash the clutch was out, so that navigation continued unchecked on the prescribed course. I pushed the rest of the way back after my momentum was exhausted, with the motor still solid. Three cheers for the lorry was my first reaction! At least I was immune from transportation problems for the homeward journey.

The winner was M.D. Whitworth, on a 348 cc Rex Acme Blackburne, at 69.96 mph, second D.A. Loveday, 348 cc Velocette, and third, A. Paul, 348 cc Velocette.

Subsequent stripping of the engine revealed no damage to the head, barrel or piston, but the flywheels and connecting rod might have been fashioned from a solid steel forging for all the movement present in the big end!

I had entered for the road races run by the Pendennis MCC at Falmouth in Cornwall, held on August bank holiday. Obviously there wasn't much time to get the damage rectified if I was to come under starter's orders. I phoned Ben Bickell and he agreed to have the engine back and do the necessary. The engine was hastily removed from the frame and stowed in the family car, a 1924 model 501 Fiat. It was delivered to Ben in Highgate and he promised to repair it and return it per passenger train. This he did, and it arrived in time for me to refix it in the frame and test the machine.

The ex-H. C. Lamacraft Velocette in grass track trim, 1934

All ready to load up for Clubman's Day, 6th April 1935

Now Bill Beamish had also entered this meeting on his Velocette, and had offered to take my machine down in his trailer, together with his brother's 250 cc TT Rudge. I had arranged to ride down on the Ariel, in company with several other local enthusiasts and we hoped to spend an enjoyable holiday in Cornwall, and have a jolly good 'blind' around Pendennis Point, on which the races were held on the bank holiday Monday.

Three of us set out for Cornwall, John 'Henry' as he preferred to be called, as no one could ever spell his real name correctly, (doubt if I could myself now!) on a 350 cc Big Port AJS; Jack Piper (who later used to act as my mechanic at Brooklands) on a 350 cc Red Hunter Ariel, and yours truly on the 499 cc Red Hunter Ariel. We had a fine uneventful run down, and arrived at a real old Cornish farm house at Helston, where John had booked the three of us in for a week's stay.

The next day, Sunday, we went along to explore the battlefield and found this to consist of nearly 2 miles of twisting tarmac roads on War Department property, with a climb on one side overlooking the harbour. The course then continued along to a hairpin bend on the Point, round the grounds of Pendennis Castle, and then dropped downhill through wooded, sweeping bends back to the start. The only straight was about 100 yards long, approached by a fast right hander, and ending in a very sharp right hander, fortunately possessing that invaluable amenity, a slip road that led downhill to the entrance to the local railway station.

We could see at once that the course would require a good deal of learning, with all those bends. Acceleration rather than flat out speed was the important factor, making it advisable to gear on the low side.

The weather was gorgeous, so we spent the day sight-seeing around the beautiful locality of Falmouth, then went for a swim to inspect some old German U boats, dumped on the rocks, and accessible at low water. Where else could you go motorcycle racing, and have the chance to wander around in a sunken U boat, inspecting the various controls, and wading through the compartments by negotiating the conveniently open watertight doors?

The Monday dawned bright and warm; this part was, after all, known as the Cornish Riviera, and palm trees grew by the side of many roads in the vicinity. After a fine farm house breakfast we made our way across the yard, dodging squealing pigs, and rescued our bikes from the barn, after having dispersed the various feathered members of the farmer's livestock who had used our machines as comfortable roosts the previous night. We didn't find any eggs laid anywhere on the bikes, but John always declared that the farm smells seeping into the innards of his AJS played no small part in his winning the races!

We were amongst the earliest competitors to arrive at the start and duly collected our numbers. I was rather concerned to learn that, so far, there was no sign of Bill Beamish and my Velocette. As time wore on, and starting time approached, my worst fears were realised. I finally encountered Bill collecting his numbers. Three machines on board was more than the trailer was prepared to stand, and it had disintegrated early in the proceedings, luckily without damage to its occupants. The Rudge and my Velo he ferried back to his shop, one at a time, then after loading his own Velo on to the back of his car, he had journeyed down to arrive just in time for the start of the meeting. He was full of apologies, but there it was. My Velocette was about 260 miles away and racing would start in about a half hour.

Falmouth 6682   Aerofilms Ltd. London

An aerial view of the Pendennis road race course at Falmouth, Cornwall *(Aerofilms Ltd)*

World War 1 German U boats on the rocks in Falmouth Bay, Cornwall, August 1934

I contacted the Clerk of the Course, and unfolded my tale of woe to him. I asked if it would be possible to ride the Ariel in the 500 cc race only. Obviously I would be a non-starter in the 350. After a hurried consultation of officials they sportingly agreed, so I dashed off to the paddock to affix the Velo's 'Senior' numbers to the former.

Upon examining the entries for the 350 race., I was very impressed by a brand new Mark IV KTT Velocette to be ridden by T.C. Whitton from Exeter. Sure enough, when the race got under way, the Velo was in the lead, and remained so for quite a while. However, he overdid things on a bend when on the climb on the far side of the course, and the Velo's crankcase came into violent contact with some Cornish granite, which proved rather unyielding. The Velocette retired forthwith, but the rider was unhurt, and pushed back to the Paddock in easy stages. No one at this stage could conceivably have known that this retirement was to prove my undoing in the next race! The Velocette's crankcase, having got the worst of the encounter with the granite, had oil dripping ominously from it. However, Whitton and his helpers worked feverishly and managed to effect temporary repairs. Unfortunately when the engine was started and the oil was delivered under pressure, some still came out.

They then decided upon one of the most assinine procedures that I ever came across in racing. Even the Velo's one gallon capacity oil tank would not be sufficient for the 500 cc race and would need replenishment. So, one of his helpers arranged to stand by the roadside with a quart tin of oil in his hand, so that somewhere after half distance, Whitton could collect this and pour it into his oil tank, without having to stop.

He evidently had some difficulty in starting the Velo in the race and I had covered several laps when to my surprise, Whitton crept by me. Knowing that he knew the course much better than I, I decided to tuck in behind him to learn his line on the corners. We bowled round that circuit in fine style for lap after lap. I couldn't pass him and he couldn't shake me off. I was thoroughly enjoying it and was gratified to know that I was lapping as fast as one of the stars.

Unknown to me the leaking oil blowing back was gradually getting on to my goggles, impairing my visibility, and the chap on the pavement daren't hold out the oil tin to him as he knew that Whitton would have to slow down in front of me to take it. At last, unable to wait any longer for oil, Whitton made a bee line for the curbing and slowed down. Not knowing what was afoot, I managed to squeeze between him and the curb as we negotiated the right hander into that straight. We must have touched just as I was getting clear and the Ariel swung broadside. I tried to correct it, but the front wheel mounted the curb. The rear wheel refused to follow and I was flung off, skating along the pavement on my backside! The bike followed me, mercifully without overhauling me! We both came to rest ultimately, and I picked myself up, relieved to find that I had no bones broken. Surprisingly, the Ariel had suffered only a bent footrest and handlebars. I managed to kick the footrest back to something approaching its normal position, but could do nothing with the handlebars. However, they were not too badly bent and I decided to continue my ride. On the next lap all traces of this little escapade had vanished, most likely all had adjourned to the Paddock, which was close by. However, the Ariel showed a reluctance to slow sufficiently for the sharp right hander, and I was overjoyed at the sight of the slip road. I could not stop it on the short downhill section and found myself in the station yard. By the courtesy of the Great Western Railway Company, that piece of their yard had been kept clear, and I was able to turn around on their property and regain the course.

I managed to finish the race without further incident, but of course, after my two escapades on the only straight part of the course, I was nowhere in the final placings.

Members of the 'local racing school' in 1934. No. 67 is the Author, 348 cc Velocette; behind him (left) Fred Snow, his mechanic; behind (right) Eric Coward (with crash helmet); (10) Stuart Stubbings 497 cc Ariel; (4) Bill Hurn 346 cc AJS; behind him (with cap) John Henry; unnumbered, Basil Keys 349 cc Rudge; (90) Jim Pether's model '90' Sunbeam and (1) T.L. Beamish 249 cc Rudge

The 350 cc race was won by John 'Henry' and his 1924 'big port' AJS, whilst another Worthing Club member, Basil Keys, making his first road racing appearance, was second on his 350 cc Rudge. In the 500 cc race they passed and re-passed, and the positions were reversed, the Rudge winning and the Ajay second. The Worthing Club also won the Team Prize, with H. Keys, brother of B.E. Keys, on a 250 cc camshaft OK Supreme, the third member.

I was gratified to learn this, and apart from a few abrasions to my person and the Ariel, we had a rewarding day out. It is interesting to recall that Basil Keys, 44 years after this, is still racing today. His son also competes.

With the help of my fellow riders, we managed to make the Ariel more comfortable to ride, the handlebars having succumbed to our combined efforts to straighten them. We spent a very enjoyable holiday in Cornwall for the rest of the week, and were sorry to leave. On the homeward run we ran into some dense holiday traffic, also returning. A bumper to bumper queue of cars stretched as far as you could see up a long hill. John was leading on the AJS whilst I brought up the rear. The AJS did not care for this treatment, and John, fearing his clutch might give out with so much slipping, got out in the middle of the road and gave the Ajay its head! Jack soon followed him, but oncoming traffic blocked my path, so I decided to stay where I was and catch them up later.

It was just as well I did. The local Constabulary had planted one of their number just over the brow of the hill, and he took exception to John's progress, and also to the voice of his AJS. He waved John in to the side of the road, and Jack followed him in. By the time I had followed the cars up to the same point the notebook had been produced, and the constable was entering particulars therein. I disclaimed any association with them and went by in the traffic stream, with no more than a passing glance. When well out of range of the constable's eagle eye I stopped to await their arrival. When we had our next stop for a break, I learned that both had been booked. Jack had waited until John had been dealt with, whereupon the notebook was clasped up and pocketed. 'Now you see where your pal did wrong' the officer said to Jack, and proceeded to lay the facts of the law before him. Jack disagreed, thinking much ado was being made about nothing, and said so in no uncertain terms. This upset the constable who decided to assert his authority, and show these 'furriners' he was not to be trifled with. The pocket was unbuttoned, the notebook produced and unfurled, and Jack's name and particulars were entered therein, along with those of the luckless John. Proceedings were ultimately taken against both, and they were duly fined, and their copybooks blotted with an endorsement apiece. I was glad that I had continued on my way, or undoubtedly my name would have found its way into that wretched notebook, to complete the hat trick. This incident was the most unfortunate of the whole trip, otherwise it had been a very enjoyable week's holiday.

It will be obvious from the foregoing that the ownership of the Velocette had done nothing to improve my racing prospects so far. However, it seemed as if the phase of bad luck had nearly run its course for there was no further Velocette trouble. Graham Walker always referred to a Velocette as 'The Veloce', and mine proved its worth, enabling me to start winning on the grass tracks in the vicinity. On the local course of the Worthing Eagle MCC it proved to be only slightly slower than Bill Beamish's ex TT mount, which was using a considerably higher compression ratio on RDI fuel. I was on PMS2, with a ratio of only about 9 1/2 to 1. At one particularly wet meeting, with the course more like a trials section than a race circuit, I swept the board, winning the 350, Unlimited, and Handicap Races, probably as a result of my trials experience.

The following year, I entered the Velocette for the 1935 Clubman's Day at Brooklands, along with my new single port Red Hunter Ariel. In the flying kilometre trials along the Railway Straight, it did not disgrace itself, to record 28 1/5 seconds a speed of 79.32 mph. The previous year my 500 cc Ariel had returned 77.14 mph. I had also entered it for the Outer Circuit and Mountain Course events, and in push starting for the former, the entire field got away, leaving me still pushing until I was exhausted, with no response from the recalcitrant motor.

Realising that it was not going to perform in this event, I discovered that there was no compression, and then that it was my own stupidity that was to blame. I had fitted a long reach racing plug on the line, after warming up, and as soon as the inlet valve had opened, it fouled the plug, driving up a slight burr on the valve and preventing it from seating. So that was that for the day, and I had reluctantly to be a non-starter. The day's racing had then to be confined to the 500 cc Ariel, as reported later. There was

40

The local grass track at Sompting in 1935. The Author congratulates Bill Hurn, 346 cc AJS, who has just beaten him in the 350 cc race

Reunited after 34 years, thanks to Jeff Clew! At the Ardingly Rally 1968

BRITISH
MOTOR CYCLE
RACING
CLUB

THE
MOTOR CYCLE

CLUBMAN'S MEETING

This is to Certify that

Mr A. C. Perryman

at Brooklands Apr. 6th 1935

riding a 348 c.c. Velocette

covered

The Flying Kilometre

in — min 28⅘ sec., a speed of

74.32 m.p.h.

Clerk of the Course.

A Brooklands Certificate, showing the time and speed recorded during the Flying Kilometre event

41

one consolation - I had finished in 4th place in these kilometre trials.

Having re-seated the valve, and thrown away the long reach plug, I settled down to grass track racing. The Sydenham MCC, having lost their fine Mountain Mile circuit at Layham's Farm, which included the 1 in 3 climb of 'Bob's Knob', had acquired a new circuit called the Flying Mile, nowhere nearly as nice as the old one, and exceedingly bumpy. Shades of Brooklands! My Velocette seemed quite at home here as the following record shows. 5th May 1935 – Bronze Medal for winning a heat. The Queen's Cup for winning the Unlimited cc Solo Handicap Race. 2nd June 1935 – Bronze Medal for winning a heat and a Silver Medal for third place in the final. 30th June 1935 was its swan song, being second in the 350 cc race and winning the Unlimited Solo, resulting in the acquisition of two silver cups. This proved to be its last outing in my hands, and I sold it to John 'Henry' of big port AJS fame. I have no record of how he fared with it, but by an extraordinary coincidence I made contact with it again 34 years later, in July 1968, at the Expo 68 Sussex exhibition held at Ardingly, Sussex.

I was there not with a motorcycle, but with a 1922 ATCO motor mower, which I had lovingly restored, and walked round with in the Grand Parade. Wandering round the Paddock I was soon attracted by an immaculate KTT and, of course, went over to inspect it. The engine number KTT266 seemed to ring a bell, and further inspection revealed a small plate attached to the rear mudguard with the legend, 'Brooklands Velocette, once owned by the late H.C. Lamacraft.' At once I recognised my old faithful, although its registration number was strangely unfamiliar, containing three letters before the numbers.

Of course, I couldn't rest until I had contacted the owner, who turned out to be none other than Jeff Clew. Jeff listened as I unfolded the cycle's history. Did he think I could just sit on it? 'Yes' I could. Of course the inevitable followed 'Do you think; could I possibly ...' 'Have a ride on it' interrupted Jeff. 'Yes you can, if you promise not to bend it' came the reply. I promised, so willing hands at the back pushed lustily and I bumped down on the saddle and let in the clutch. The motor responded instantly, and sounded gorgeous. The old familiar note exuded from the Brooklands can! I revelled in that melody which had not assailed my ears for the last 30 years! I caused the machine to gyrate on the greensward, and it still felt like the thoroughbred that it was. I managed to refrain from bending it, returning it to Jeff in one piece, albeit rather reluctantly.

Jeff told how he had found it, acquired same and rebuilt it. The only thing not original was the petrol tank, and the front forks. The original had the large type of TT tank and strutted Webb forks. He had been unable to acquire either of these and had perforce to incorporate those as used on the standard KSS model of that era. I understand that he has since acquired the proper forks. That left the question of the registration numbers. I had a photo of it taken when I had acquired it originally, complete with front number plate, newly repainted for Clubman's Day 1934! Jeff borrowed the photograph, and with a covering letter from me the licensing authorities graciously restored the machine's original registration numbers. I understand that it has since re-visited the Isle of Man and had a canter along part of the Mountain road closed specially for the occasion – the Golden Jubilee of the Manx Grand Prix.

In our local circus of racing participants was a certain local builder, whom I will identify by his christian name, Ernie. We envied him, in as much as he was not under the financial handicap of the majority of us, and was able to go about in a Hillman straight eight. Ernie thought he would like to impress his numerous lady friends (he never seemed to be without the company of some exotic bird) by racing a motorcycle, so he acquired a **brand new** Mark IV KTT Velocette, complete with spare sprint petrol tank, dope piston, sprockets etc., - a complete racing ensemble. One of the local dealers, Tom Fassett, supplied the machine and looked after it. All Ernie had to do was **ride** it!

Every meeting he took it to, something happened and I cannot remember it finishing a race. Tom even went up to Brooklands with it as Ernie coveted a Gold Star, but he only managed to creep round near the tail end of the field.

After about 12 months of this, Ernie could see that, far from enhancing his prestige in the eyes of the feminine community, it was probably doing just the reverse! So he decided to dispose of the unfortunate Velocette, engine No. KTT514. 'That bike's a bloody Jonah' he wailed. 'No blighter will ever do anything with it, except kill or injure himself.' So, one fine day, I was surprised to see it standing in the line of bikes for sale, outside Bill Beamish's establishment, the other local dealer, as I passed by. I

Driving side of 'The Jonah'

Success at the first
outing; a 2nd place in the
Clubman's Junior Mountain
Championship on 27th July
1935

In the lead, Clubman's
Junior GP, 31st August 1935

43

stopped right away, retraced my steps, and asked Bill if I was seeing things, or was it really for sale? 'S's right' said Bill, 'you know how Ernie feels about it; he'll take fifty quid for the lot, lock, stock and barrel.' I couldn't believe it, only twelve months old and now well under half price. 'It's mine' I gasped, hardly able to get the words out. 'Here's a quid deposit on it, it's all I have on me'. Not only all I had on me, but all I had in the world as regards cash! I had no idea of how I would acquire the next £49 but I was certain that I'd raise it somehow during the next few days.

'Hope you know what you're taking on' Bill cautioned. 'I wouldn't touch it with a barge pole; you must be a bigger bloody fool than I thought you were.' My mind was firmly made up. 'I'll chance that, Bill. I don't intend to use any barge poles or similar inducements on it, I plan to **ride** it.' Bill was adamant. 'You can't take it away until you've settled in full for it. That's my orders. Why, you might even kill yourself on the bloody thing before you get it home.' 'OK Bill, I'll be along with the balance within a week; in the meantime don't let anyone buy it over my head.' With that I took my leave of him, to concentrate on my next headache, the forty nine pounds! In those days it was a respectable sum to anyone. You could purchase a house for £25 down and about 10 shillings a week. To anyone of my financial prospects, it was an astronomical amount. Every avenue I explored drew the same answer. 'And when do you think I'll see it back?' I could no more answer that than could the person posing the question. At last I plucked up enough courage to ask my own father, after explaining how I would love to get astride that Mark IV, and he kindly agreed to advance the necessary, even though he knew the same as I, that he might never see the return of it.

With the crisp notes in my pocket, I collected young Fred Snow, who always came to grass track meetings with me, and together we went along on my Ariel, armed with a tow rope and cardboard plate emblazoned with the legend **on tow**, and the Ariel's number beneath. The plate was duly attached to the rear of Fred's person, and the rope from the Ariel to the Velocette. The crisp notes had already changed hands, and in their place I had my official receipt and the Velo's log book. The pannier bags that had nearly met an early demise en route to the Isle of Man took care of the bits and pieces, having previously been secured to the Ariel's nether quarters.

Bill wished me luck, asked what flowers I liked best, and said he felt relieved the machine was off his premises. With Fred's help in the steering department, it reached my little garage safely. As I had suspected all along, the bad name the Velo had acquired was completely unjustified, and it proved to be one of the finest mounts I ever had. I never took it out without winning something. It gained at least a place in every event in which I entered it, and proved one of the fastest Velocettes of the Mark IV variety. I raced it for about two years and then sold it to Eric Oliver, who became the South Eastern Centre's Grass Track Champion with it!

It was Bill Beamish who persuaded me eventually to part with it, saying that it was now getting old, and I should acquire something later and faster. I always regretted this, and was confident that had I have tried, I could have got a 350 cc Gold Star with it at Brooklands, had I picked the right day weatherwise.

In later years I got to know Brooklands Velocette ace Les Archer, and we were discussing how to make Velo's go fast. Les, of course, sold them, and he confided to me that one of the most frequent queries he dealt with from prospective clients was, 'How do you make them go really quickly.' Les's reply was classic, and very much to the point. 'You do two things' he told them all. 'You sit on it, and you open it right out.' I often chuckled about this remark, and I think KTT514 fully bore out Les's philosophy.

I acquired the Mark IV just in time to enter the forthcoming Clubmen's Junior Mountain Championship at Brooklands on 27th July 1935. I had already entered the Ariel in the Senior Race and looked forward to a fine day's racing. The usual lorry load of supporters materialised, and off we went to the track. I had only the morning of the race in which to practice so I concentrated on the Velo, not being as familiar with it as I was with the Ariel. This was my first outing on it, and it did not take me long to establish that the gear change was not all that it should be. I missed several changes, feeling a proper Charlie in doing so, but luckily no damage accrued to the power plant, or so I thought. However, even a Velocette will not indefinitely accept the over revving entailed with clumsy gear changes, and the exhaust valve and piston embraced each other. But the machine continued to circulate quite rapidly, and I was unaware that anything was amiss.

We all duly lined up for the Junior Championship race; my number was 1 and I hoped to justify this. Being of powerful stature, and going the best part of 14 stone in racing gear, I always prided myself in being amongst the very first into the first corner, if not the first. This time it was different; the Velo refused to fire! I rocked it back against compression whilst the rest of the field receded into the distance. It was then that I realised I had bent the valve in practice, as I could not find compression. I realised only a superhuman effort, and a long, fast run would bring that motor to life, and set about the task in earnest. The remarks about the Jonah came searing through my mind, and I determined to lay it once and for all. Luck was with me and the motor coughed and spluttered a bit before taking hold, as I climbed aboard to make a belated entry into the first corner – in the tail position.

I was unaccustomed to being in this position and set about rectifying matters without delay. Once I got the revs up the motor responded magnificently, and with no one around me at the moment, I began to circulate quite rapidly, the bent valve apparently making but scant difference to the motor's power potential. After a few laps I began to overhaul the stragglers and in spite of another missed gear on leaving the fork, I was moving rapidly through the field. The leaders were still a long way ahead though, and I realised that in the ten available laps, I would not catch D. Wells on his 344 cc Excelsior, which was fitted with a racing JAP engine. Just before the finish, however, the second man, D.J. Maloney, came to grief on his Velocette, when he touched the leader on a corner at the Member's Hill turn. This let me up into second place, and I could see Wells now not so far ahead. If I could have been first instead of last into that first corner, the Velo would most likely have won its first race. Third was Dennis Loveday on his Velocette. The winner's speed was 62.86 mph.

Upon reading C.K. Mortimer's excellent book on Brooklands, I was interested to learn of how he made his racing pay by playing the bookies. No such luck came my way. One of my supporters tried to place a bet on me, in both the Junior and Senior events. The bookie refused to take it, and was cheerfully calling out his odds and concluding with 'Anyone bar Perryman', so my colleague informed me.

Back at home, I decided that as all sorts of people had been playing around with this cycle, and heaven knows what they had been up to, I would return both power plant and gearbox to Hall Green for attention, so having a fresh start for my next outing. Both units were carefully packed in stout boxes and turned over to the servants of the Southern Railway, for despatch to Hall Green. They were not away long, and eventually were re-delivered to my home one day by the ever faithful shire horse and vintage van.

The motor has been reassembled with its petrol piston, all I had used so far, as dope was barred in the Clubman's races. My sights were now set on the Junior Clubman's Grand Prix, due to take place at Brooklands on 31st August.

Included in the spares I had acquired was a spare straight-through exhaust pipe of correct length for racing, and anxious to hear the Velo's voice with this, I reassembled with it, and started the motor. It sounded glorious, and it also looked fine, with its large TT tank and racing fittings. I could not resist taking a photo of it with my somewhat ancient and elementary *No 2 Brownie* camera.

How nice it would be to take it over to the Isle of Man for the TT I thought. Better to erase such thoughts from the mind, t'ain't even paid for yet counselled my inner self. It was well on the way though, thanks to the proceeds of the sale of KTT266 and sundry other sums which had swelled into the kitty as the result of my efforts to extract a few more mph from the mounts of several of the local aspirants to racing honours. Anyway, why the Isle of Man? What's wrong with the local A 27 thought I? That's it! I would rise very early one fine Sunday morning and do my best to emulate Stanley Woods. I thought it prudent though, to substitute the shorter pipe and Brooklands can for the straight through variety, and to reinstate the registration numbers front and rear.

The absence of any of the requisite road fund documents at the time, however, entirely escaped my notice. It was hoped that the exercise would be completed and the cycle interned in its stall, before the local Constabulary was astir. There were very few mobile patrols about in those days, and such as were would be unlikely to keep the Velocette in sight for very long! The idea appealed immensely, and as the very next Saturday was a perfect summer day, I watched the sun go down, and my local weather lore persuaded me that the morrow would dawn equally fine. I hied me off to the land of nod, so that I could arise with the sun on the morrow and hold a TT on my own.

Sure enough, my weather forecast proved more reliable than the weather centre expert's variety of the present day, and I was awake before old King Sol had cleared the horizon. I climbed into my racing leathers, conveniently laid out the previous evening to be immediately accessible, and crept stealthily downstairs, knee boots in hand so as not to disturb the other members of the parental household. Once outside the house I donned boots, helmet, goggles and gloves, and made my way as silently as possible to where my trusty steed awaited me. I was so excited I fumbled with the lock on the stable door for what seemed an age to me, but at last it yielded to my efforts, and I eased the Velo off its stand and into the road. The stable door now bolted, the horse and I being on the right side of it, I turned on the fuel and rocked the Velo back on compression. A heave, surprisingly few purposeful paces, and bump into the saddle. The Velo responded immediately - it was obviously as anxious as I to sample the joys of deserted roads on this heavenly summer morning. Steady now, for a little while until we clear the houses. The locals will take a very poor view of being awakened at 3.30 am on a Sunday morning by the Velo's blatent exhaust. The houses are well clear now, so not too many revs. and into second. Same again and into third, and finally top. The morning air is whistling past my cheeks now, cool, fresh, and wonderfully pure. In no time at all I had reached the outskirts of the conurbation of Brighton and Hove. It would be inadvisable to proceed much further eastwards, as this was sure to result in a brush with the local constabulary, and that would never do! So, down through the gears, use those TT brakes, and execute now what is officially called a U turn. Once more, up through the gears, heading back towards home. Straight open road now, time to sit back on the pad and lay along the tank. No speedometer or rev. counter on this animal, but my experience tells me that we're doing nearly ninety.

I soon run out of road at this gait, and all too soon the unwelcome sight of houseroofs appears ahead. Don't antagonise the locals, so ease back that throttle and line up for that fast right hander ahead, which will take us on to the A 283 to Horsham, a road of decidedly more rural aspect, offering some excellent cornering prospects. Into third, into second, lay it over and open the taps. The Velo goes round as if it were on rails. Easy now, there's another right hander ahead. Into third for a short straight ahead, line up for the fast left hander, use ALL the road this time; Stanley would! Now's the time for peak revs. in third; the straight ahead rejoices in the name of Madman's Mile, and should just about accept peak revs in top, let alone third. Good, we've made that peak in top, but back into third now, there's some tricky bends about for a couple of miles. Won't be needing top any more outward bound, as the village of Bramber lies ahead, and after sampling the joys of crossing Ballaugh Bridge, the famous Isle of Man hazard, (our Sussex version is known as Beeding Bridge and will have to deputise for its I.O.M. counterpart this morning as it's even more hunchbacked than the real article) it will be advisable to shut off early, and as soon as we've landed, it will mean another U turn and leg it for home. Crunch - the forks bottom on landing. I took that quite fast enough; I've never been airborne for such a distance previously at that point.

Never mind, now turn the cycle round and get out of this peaceful village! Not too much twist grip until we're out in the open once more. Now we're clear, and ready to enjoy the high speed swervery all the way back to Madman's Mile. There's the Mile coming up now, into top after the fast right hander. Good! farmer Frampton's cows are still grazing in the field, so there will be no slimy trail of cow dung through the fast right hander as there was when I once tried to take the Ariel through at about eighty! That trip nearly ended in disaster; luckily the road was empty as I slid from side to side. No such hazard today, Frampton hasn't yet arrived to drive them down to his milking stalls. Easy now. Gently on that throttle and use all the road once more. Fine; even Stanley might have approved of my navigation this morning. Less than half a mile before the stable door now. Kill the motor and coast home, no need to wake everyone up. That's it for today, as feet touch terra firma once more. Stow the cycle away in its stall now and lock up. Phew it's going to be a scorcher today. Get out of those leathers, have a freshening up wash, and then a nice hot cup of tea. Ah that's better. Now I can appreciate how Stanley and Co feel after their early morning practice. What's the time by the way? 4.45 am. Good gracious! another couple of hours to go before breakfast time. I'll go back and remove the flies impaled on the gallant Velocette after its early morning canter. I sit down on an empty two gallon petrol can and lazily start to clean up the Velo. No oil leaks; the motor went perfectly. Oh, and I almost forgot, I never once missed a gear. They went in like a hot knife slicing through butter. Those people at Hall Green have done a good job. Should stand a good chance in the Grand Prix on 31st August.

The regulations for Clubmen demanded that all machines should be equipped with a kickstarter, but not necessarily started by same; you could push start if you wished. The TT gearbox as fitted to a KTT carried no such encumberance. A friend of mine, Eric Coward, owned a KSS model of a similar vintage and this possessed what was needed. Eric sportingly removed the complete gearbox end cover from his box. I did likewise and we exchanged them! The kickstarter operated through teeth on the face of the 1st gear pinion, the KSS and KTT models having a different number of teeth. Short of changing the complete gear clusters or complete boxes,, there was no way of making the kickstarter work. I needed the close ratios of the KTT's box, so we decided that the kickstarter would have to be present in name only and both of us would have to push start.

The day duly dawned and both Ariel and Velocette were loaded on the lorry before we headed for Brooklands. People such as myself were at a distinct disadvantage compared to the more fortunate mortals who either lived in the vicinity, or better still rented a shed on the premises, and could try out their settings at any time, to make any modifications deemed desirable. In my case, I could practice only on the morning of the event, and then with two machines of completely different characteristics. If anything was not right, about all I could do in the available time would be to change jets, plugs, or at most, ignition settings or gear ratios.

And so it proved to be for the Junior Grand Prix. As I so often found at Brooklands, the wind was against me along the Railway Straight. I took the Velo out first, with its standard IOM gearing that required a 23 tooth gearbox sprocket. It went very well, but it seemed to labour along that Railway Straight, and pick up about halfway round the Byfleet Banking, as it came round out of the wind. It was fine along the Finishing Straight, but here were placed two different sets of oil drums to simulate artificial bends to reproduce road racing conditions; high speed here would be of much less advantage. Speed on the Railway Straight was essential if you wanted to win, and who didn't? Plodding along that Straight, tucking my large bulk away as best I could, I was passed by Les Archer on his Velocette, going very well. I was surprised to see him right over the far side underneath the shelter of the Railway Company's bank and fencing. Right, I thought! What's good enough for Les is good enough for me, and I went over there as well. It certainly gave some protection, and I think progress was marginally better, but still not good enough.

I rode back into the Paddock and turned it over to Jack Piper. 'Put the 22 tooth sprocket on Jack, whilst I take out the Ariel' I said. 'She's a dead duck against the wind.' The Ariel didn't seem to mind the wind to the same extent and I put in a few laps with it, deciding that I would leave it as it was, and made for the Paddock once more, intending to put in some more laps with the Velo. But time was running out, and before I could get through the gate to the track it was closed. Practice time was over. Vickers wanted to get aircraft out over to the aerodrome. Nothing for it but to chance it with the 22 tooth sprocket. Pits were provided by the trackside in this race, as in the IOM. Fred Snow and Jack Piper would occupy mine, and I planned to go flat out along the Railway Straight but ease off on the other side to keep the revs. within safe limits, provided I could get in the lead and remain unchallenged. Unknown to me, my pit (No 29) was very close to the barrels marking the corners, so when approaching I could not see them, requiring all my concentration for lining up to take the best course through the barrels. When the flag fell, the Velo responded nobly and I was first into the first corner this time. I tucked in along the straight, under the bank, eased off when the revs. got too high on the other side, and swept through the barrels in fine style. To quote *The Motor Cycle* report. 'In the lead was A.C. Perryman on a healthy sounding Velocette.' No one appeared to challenge me and I reeled off lap after lap, always easing for the down wind side of the course. Every lap I looked down the pit line as long as I dared, but I could not see Fred before I had to return my gaze to the track ahead. Fred was doing all he knew to attract my attention, telling me to get a move on! Unbeknown to me, Dennis Loveday, having made a very bad start on an older type of Velocette, had now got moving, and was rapidly narrowing the distance between us.

For ten laps I went my own sweet way, in the lead, and then on lap eleven, Dennis came by me just as I was easing off, coming round the Byfleet Banking. I immediately opened up the Velo and it responded, leaving Dennis behind. He told me afterwards, 'I did not know what would happen if I eventually passed you, and when you drew away again I thought, that's torn it, he's still got some in the bag.' Dennis had worked it out beforehand that if he could deal with me, the race was his. I knew now

Clubman's Junior GP 1935. The Author, 348 cc Velocette (39), prepares to pass Dennis Loveday, 348 cc Velocette (35), as they leave the first set of oil drum markers *(Motor Cycle)*

Clubman's Junior GP, 31st August 1935. Dennis Loveday frantically tucks away in a vain effort to prevent the Author from passing him whilst the latter gets too close to an oil drum and hurriedly leans away from it. Dennis won, with the Author (39) a close second, both riding 348 cc Velocettes *(Motor Cycle)*

that there would be no more easing off. I'd just have to let the Velo go, and hope it would hang together. Having shaken him off I thought the danger was over, and was dismayed to find Dennis coming by once more, towards the end of the Railway Straight. He was over the other side getting no shelter from the bank, but still drawing away from me. Matters were evened up once more as we came off the Byfleet Banking, the Mk IV being considerably the faster with the wind, and so it went on every lap. At last I realised the awful truth. Dennis was getting more on me along the straight than I could make up on the other side, owing to the barrels! I was regaining the lead later every lap. As the start and finish was on the side where I led, I prayed that I would be able to hold him off, or at worst re-pass him just before the line. But it was not to be. With two laps to go, Dennis managed to get into the corner just before two slower riders that we had both lapped. I was less fortunate. They took up all the course between them, and I had to brake violently to avoid running them down. By the time I got the chance to clear them, Dennis was well away and I never caught him again. He won by seven seconds, and thoroughly deserved his win. It had been a great scrap! If only I could have seen Fred's frantic signals on those first ten laps I could easily have saved two seconds a lap and the positions would then have been reversed. The Velo showed no signs of distress in spite of the low gear. I could have saved a couple of seconds each lap without driving it to dangerous revs. But it was Dennis's day. Third was D. Wells, on his 344 cc Excelsior JAP. It is interesting to note that these were the same three as in the Mountain Championship results a month earlier. The first and third men changed places and I remained second! The winner's speed was 72.16 mph.

The Grand Prix concluded the Brooklands programme for 1935 as far as I, a clubman, was concerned. The Senior event is dealt with later, in my chapter on the Ariel's adventures.

The time had now arrived to change my 'Jonah' Velocette over to alcohol fuel, and see what I could do with it on the grass. Unlike some of the regular Brooklands habitues, I was never able to afford the luxury of separate alcohol and petrol machines, or even engines. I had to change mine over from one to the other, as required. Maybe it was not the best policy, but it was the only one open to me. The local grass track at Sompting afforded a chance to try out alcohol fuel and I managed to win the 350 cc class, and secure a place in both the Unlimited and Handicap races. At a subsequent meeting one member, Bill Hurn, had just acquired a new camshaft 350 cc AJS, and try as I would I could not pass him. I had to be content with second place this time, and congratulated him when we got back in the Paddock on having such a fine machine. My policy from now on was to use the Velocette only for the 350 cc events, the Unlimited and Handicap Races being left to the 500 cc Ariel, which by now was almost uncatchable.

1935 had been my most successful season so far. I had proved that the Mark IV would deliver the goods if it were treated kindly. But I was still not satisfied with it. The humiliating experience with Bill Hurn's AJS, and also its dislike of the wind along the Railway Straight, decided me to have it right down during the off season to see if I could wring a few more mph from it, and in particular, cure its dislike of a headwind.

As the works had already overhauled the engine, I could not think of any improvements I could carry out there, so I decided to start with the camshaft housing. I stripped this right out, and found that both the cams and the rockers, the latter of which bore directly on the cams, showed signsof wear. Thinking that I might be loosing some valve lift, and possibly have late opening and early closing, I decided to renew the lot. Now the Mark IV, according to the spares list, carried a No. 30 cam, and mine was so stamped on one of the cam lobes. I sent the order off to Hall Green, and the spares duly arrived. The replacement cam had no number of any sort on it, and would not go onto the camshaft. I took it along to the works with me, and one of our millwrights fixed me up with a split lap. I got to work on the offender with this and some grinding paste (the cam was very hard), and at last was able to force it onto the shaft. It was almost tight enough to dispense with the key, but needless to say, I didn't! Upon re-assembly, the degree plate was fixed on the crankshaft, and the timing checked against the works figures for the No 30 cam. I couldn't believe my eyes. The figures I got were nothing like it. There was no question of an error in assembling the bevel gear. The valves were opening **before** they should do and closing later, inlet and exhaust the same.

I checked with other local Velocette riders. They could all get the figures quoted by the works. Clearly, the cam supplied to me was not a No 30, but what the heck WAS it? Maybe a **real** IOM TT cam, or a dirt track one? Velo's had made a few machines for the dirt track business, but I did not like to write and ask the works for fear they asked for its return, and sent me a proper No 30 in lieu thereof.

No, I would try the machine out with it. If it was worse I would replace it with a proper No 30. But who knows? I might have a **very** rapid Velocette. I also had my doubts about that exhaust pipe I had inherited from Ernie, to which the silencer was attached. All other Brooklands Velos used a much longer pipe than mine, particularly Dennis Loveday's. The works kindly furnished figures plotting maximum bhp against pipe lengths, and according to my calculations, the pipe was miles out! I cut the long racing pipe to the new length I had calculated to give me the best results, and ordered a new straight-through pipe to replace the cut down one. Let's have a fresh start I decided. I now treated with suspicion anything that I had acquired with the cycle from Ernie!

The regulations for Clubman's Day 1936 appeared in *The Motor Cycle*. Anyone who had gained a first, second or third in any previous Clubman's race would not be eligible to compete again. This was indeed a blow. No Brooklands for me. Much later, when eventually I joined the BMCRC, I learned from Duncan Ferguson that this regulation had been introduced especially for my benefit. Their version was that, if anyone was good enough to gain a win or place, they were good enough to become a regular Bemsee member!

I immediately stripped the Velo's engine. It was alcohol from now on. I might never need that petrol piston again. The only two places requiring its use, the IOM and Brooklands, for Clubman's events, were now out of my reach, albeit for different reasons. I decided to take the Velo up to the Sunbeam MCC's sprint at the Gatwick Speed Trials, along with the Ariel. The results of this are given in a later chapter.

Its next outing was at our local grass track, and it looked as if this and Gatwick would be its only outlets in future.

At the first local grass track meeting, I had the satisfaction of showing a clean pair of heels to Bill Hurn and his AJS. He was not to get the better of my Velo from now on, and I began to feel that my efforts over the winter had been worth while.

The next thing to occur was a pleasant surprise. The regulations for the Clubman's Grand Prix at Brooklands came out, and there was no restrictive clause. I lost no time in entering both my machines and set about changing them over to petrol, and making sure there was no repetition of last year's mistakes. Several times the Velo had shown a tendency to oil up plugs on the grass tracks. At the Motor Cycle Show last winter I had taken this up with KLG Plugs, and they recommended their No 690 so I purchased one. I had always used a Lodge BR 51 up till now. I had not yet used this 690, so decided to keep it for the Grand Prix on 18th July.

When the day arrived I straight away took out the Velo, to see if my efforts of last winter had improved it on this circuit. I was pleasantly surprised. This time it made no bones about the Railway Straight, in spite of pulling its correct 23 tooth sprocket. Remember, I had to substitute a 22 tooth last year. It was miles an hour faster, and I put in several good laps, getting so worked up that I came a purler and dropped it in negotiating the barrels. I picked it up, kicked the footrest straight, and carried on immediately, as I didn't want to lose my nerve. Everything seemed fine; it was appreciably faster than last year, the cam or the longer pipe, or both, had certainly enhanced its performance.

The regulations this year required each entrant to provide a lap scorer. Geoff Griffiths, a fellow member of the Brighton and District MCC and another Velocette owner, had come along to attend to this for me. There was to be no more invisible pit signals either. Fred Snow was to be stationed up in the lattice supports of the bridge across the track, near the Paddock gates. This had the advantage that he was easily visible, as I would have finished negotiating the barrels, and could look over at him as I accelerated away. Jack Piper would be in the pit booth as usual, but there would not be much point in pulling in there in a 50 mile race. If you did, there would not be much chance of a place in the race. After a warm up, the KLG 690 was fitted. I put my trusty old BR 51 in my pocket. It might save me a long walk home if the worst happened. We were ushered out on the track and lined up at the start. This year I was No 39 as against 29 last year. Dennis Loveday was not in the event this year. He had already joined BMCRC so there would be no scrap with him. We all rocked our machines back against compression, then the flag fell.

With a mighty heave and the minimum number of paces, I flung my weight on the saddle. The motor fired immediately, accelerating like a rocket as I swung myself aboard. There was a sharp left

The line up at the start of an Outer Circuit handicap race on 23rd May 1936. Duncan Ferguson, the Secretary, is in the trilby hat and light raincoat, with his hands in his pockets. Eric Fernihough, scratch man, is on the extreme left, to the left of the letter 'A' *(Motor Cycle)*

hander about 200 yards from the start, leading out on to the outer circuit. I shut off and lined up for this, then at the right moment, opened up to pull the Velo round and away towards the Railway Straight. To my horror, nothing happened. The motor was as dead as mutton. That 690 had oiled up on the first bend. So great was the lead built up in that first 200 yards that I had reached the inside of the track, dismounted, and got the Velo on its stand before the rest came by. No time to lose now. Off with gloves, take out that wretched 690, then my faithful BR 51 from my pocket and get it into the head. My fingers seemed all thumbs in my towering rage over this completely unexpected turn of events. At last the 51 was in position, the offender returned to my pocket, gloves on, off stand, rock back onto compression and heave! None too soon either; I could hear the exhausts of the leaders coming up to start their next lap. No time to look round to see who they are, that oiled up plug would have cost me a lap by the time I've got up to their speed.

Was I pleased to hear that once again the power plant was functioning normally. It would henceforth have to give every ounce it could produce if I was to stand any hope of a place, as each lap would occupy over two minutes, a hell of a lot to make up in 50 miles, even on a Velocette. One consolation; I would have the track to myself for a few laps, so no one would impede me through the barrels until later on. I also did not need to look at Fred for signals. There was only one needed today, 'Get a move on' Thankfully the BR 51 showed no signs of emulating the 690, and I circulated rapidly for several laps, the power plant now on its best behaviour. I could see the tail end of the field. At least I should not be last; I passed three on that last lap. They appeared almost to be standing still.

One competitor stands out in my mind even today. He was mounted on a Royal Enfield and had a maroon coloured helmet perched almost on the back of his head. He was the first one I caught up with, and after that I seemed to overhaul him about every third lap! I lost count of the number of times I passed him. The Velo had arrived now with a vengeance. There seemed to be motorcycles everywhere. Damn. Those two are right on my line through those bends. Have to ease a bit until we're through, then get out of their way.

Unknown to me, another little drama was being enacted opposite the lap scoring box. Each scorer had a set of cardboard numbers in a frame in front of him, with 0 outermost. As his rider passed, each scorer transferred that number to the back of the stack. Geoff's score was the lowest of all, I was almost a lap behind. As he removed number 4 displaying 5, an irate gentleman in plus fours leapt out of the

51

timing box, grabbed a megaphone, and bawled across the track, 'Number 39, put back No 4, you moved two numbers last time.' Geoff was surprised. He was sure he hadn't. He shook his head at him, indicating that he wasn't going to comply. The irate gent was adamant. 'Move that number back, or we disqualify No 39.' he bawled out through his megaphone. That was the last thing Geoff wanted. I'd had a bad enough time already, and at least I was getting a ride now. I managed to glance over to Fred as I went under the bridge next time. He was grinning all over his face, and waving his arm furiously from side to side, 'Get moving'. I was! Every lap I passed more and more of the entry. On one lap, about three quarter distance, I must have passed at least ten, not counting the regular on the Enfield. Can't be many more ahead now I thought, I must be near the front, but still I passed some more. At last the man with the chequered flag; he waved it at me, I eased off and rode into the Paddock. Fred was there to greet me. He thumped me on the back, 'Well done' he bawled in my ear. 'But why did you do that extra lap?' 'What extra lap' I asked, now off the Velo and helmet removed. By now Geoff had arrived, breathless, from his lap scoring. 'They made you do an extra lap' he managed to get out, in between gasping for breath. 'That's what I told him' chimed in Fred. A small group of people now surrounded us. They all agreed. They had been watching, particularly, as the Velo cleaved its way back through the field. One was a Bemsee member. 'If I were you chum, I'd go along to the Timekeepers' Box and check up. I'm sure you did one too many. Get your bike out and go down and see 'em. I would.' They can't all be wrong I thought, so I started the Velo, and made for the Paddock gate. It was closed, a large figure in the shape of Ted Baragwanath, Chief Marshal, holding it. 'And where the 'ell d'yr think yer going', Ted ('Barry' to you) demanded. 'Up to the timekeepers, to see why I've done a lap too many' I blurted out.

A typical 'period' advertisement taken from a pre-war Brooklands programme. Records attained at the track are used to provide evidence of a tuner's ability.

Clubman's Junior GP, 18th July 1936. Pulling back the lap lost at the start, the Author, 348 cc Velocette sweeps by R.M. Beard (1) 248 cc Excelsior and L.A. Pitts (30) 348 cc Velocette to finish third and make a record lap at 77.17 mph *(Motor Cycle)*

C.K. Mortimer, winner of the Senior Mountain Championship, at 70.43 mph on 27th July 1935 *(Motor Cycle)*

'Heard that one before' said 'Barry'. 'Listen mate, the timekeepers never make a mistake, go away!' The Bemsee member sprang to my defence. 'Honest Barry, I'm sure he did. There's quite a few witnesses too'. They argued between them for a while. Barry relented. 'All right, hurry up, next race due in half an hour', and with that he opened the gate to release me.

Arriving at the Timekeepers Box, I parked the Velo and went inside. They all looked up in surprise. 'What's the trouble?' 'I did a lap too many' I gasped. They all looked from one to the other. One spoke up, the irate gent in plus fours. 'No 39 are you' he queried? 'That's right' said I hopefully. 'Your lap scorer made a mistake. I had to correct him' he said cynically. Ebby, the Chief Timekeeper, was slowly making his way over to the gent's seat. 'Let's see your sheet' he demanded. The gent stood to one side so that Ebby might see, and I peered over his shoulder. Ebby read out aloud, "Lap 1 -, Lap 2 - 2 mins 2 secs, Lap 3 -, Lap 4, - Lap 4: Why, you've entered lap 4 twice. The man's quite right, he **must** have done a lap too many' 'So what happens now?' I asked of Ebby who was looking at the irate gent with extreme displeasure, the latter's face having taken on rather a ruddy complexion. 'We deduct your last lap time from your total race time.' The irate gent was not to be outdone. 'I don't suppose that will affect anything' he exclaimed. 'Oh, but it does' cut in Ebby, 'It brings this man up into third place.' That rather cheered me up. Another few laps and I'm sure the Velo would have made it. I had been busy reading my lap times over Ebby's shoulder. My second was my fastest, 2 mins 2 secs, when I had the track to myself. I can't remember the others, but they weren't much slower.

Arriving back in the Paddock, I relayed the good news and everyone felt better. We checked on that 2 minutes 2 seconds against the lap speeds given in the programme. Nearly 78 mph! The race had been won by Johnny Lockett on a Manx Norton, at 71.01 mph. Second man was E.R. Taylor, also on a 348 cc Norton. Third myself, 348 cc Velocette. This was 1.15 mph slower than last year's event because a gale, gusting to 50 mph, was blowing against us along the Railway Straight. If I hadn't have lengthened my exhaust pipe, I should most likely have had to get off and push!

Besides the Clubman's race of course, there was a 100 mile Grand Prix for the Experts. George Rowley, on a 'works' AJS, won this. Speed? Just over 76 mph. My Velo had shown enough speed to win not only the Junior Clubman's but to finish well up in the Experts as well. That wretched 690 plug had cost me the race, so for the second year running the Grand Prix had eluded me.

Although I did not know it at the time, this was to be the last time I ever rode a Velocette at Brooklands. I always regretted that I let Bill Beamish persuade me to part with it. I joined Bemsee only a matter of weeks after this day's racing, as I had got the message that it was definitely the finis for me, as far as Clubman's events were concerned; I was very definitely barred!

Had I persevered, there was a very good chance of me gaining a 350 Gold Star with the Velo, given a suitable day. The new cam and the longer pipe had very considerably increased its performance, and I might have got even more in time. Les Archer held the 350 cc lap record at this time, at 104 mph - on a 348 cc Velocette similar to mine. (Engine No. KTT411).

Chapter Five

Help from Ariel Motors

I went as a spectator to the Senior Grand Prix held at Brooklands on 28th July 1934. In the Paddock I met Ben Bickell astride a magnificent single port Ariel Red Hunter complete with bronze head. Ben informed me that this model would be a standard production model next year, but without the bronze head. I was very impressed with it and it seemed to motor well in Ben's capable hands, although he retired after about six laps. He was second on it in 1936. As the weeks passed, more and more I thought of acquiring one myself. At the Motor Cycle Show held near the end of the year, I had another look at one on the Ariel stand and got into conversation with Len Heath, one of the star trials riders of those days, who always rode Ariels. Len was full of praise for the new model. I told him I wished to enter trials and also to race it, and had been using one of the 4 valve 500 cc models, on which I had managed to win a 2nd Class Award in the South Eastern Centre's Southern Trial. Len looked very surprised. 'Good God' he said, 'If you could win a 2nd class on one of those bloody things, you'd get the Premier Award on one of these'. 'What's up with them then, don't you like them Len?' I asked. 'Like 'em! I came as near to killing myself on one as I've done on any bike. I refuse to ride one', was the reply. Seeing someone he knew on the other side of the stand, Len seized the chance to get away from me. Maybe he thought that he might get asked to take my 4 valve model in part exchange, and they obviously were not exactly his favourite model! As far as I was concerned, that clinched the matter. I would treat myself to a new Red Hunter for 1935, and as soon as I was back home, I went along to see Bill Beamish, to see if he could do a deal with me.

Bill agreed to take my present model for a very fair price, so the order was duly placed. The only thing I didn't like about the new model was the top feed to the carburettor. I asked Bill to get me one fitted with a TT 34 racing carburettor having a bottom feed. This he did, and I took delivery on New Year's Day 1935, saying goodbye to my old 4 valver of so many episodes. The new model carried the engine No. KA781.

The programme for the new Ariel was quite hectic. It had to be run-in, and then it would be entered for 3 really tough trials, after which it would have to be taken down, ready for its debut at Brooklands for Clubman's Day, on 6th April.

The running-in had to take place in the evenings, after I got home from the works, and at week-ends. In its first trial I was very pleased with its handling and I won a 1st Class Award. In the second trial I again won a 1st Class Award and was a member of the winning team. The last of the three was the best of all. Here it annexed the Premier Award, and once more, I was a member of the winning team. It then had to be withdrawn from trials events with some urgency, as Clubman's Day was fast approaching. It had covered some 850 miles so the engine was stripped, all the trials mud cleaned off the cycle parts, and everything cleaned up and adjusted. Nothing needed renewal. I had obtained two exhaust pipes with it, one upswept for trials use and the other downswept for racing, both using the same silencer. The latter was fitted and the machine was taken out for test. I returned a speedometer reading of 95 mph along my favourite stretch of road, but I did not have much faith in this reading, after my experience at Brooklands the previous year.

The South England Ariel stronghold in 1934. L to R E.J. (Joe) Heath 349 cc BSA, Len Heath 497 cc Ariel, Graham Oates on the outfit to promote Empire Goods, Isle of Man to Canada

We went in the lorry as usual, the Ariel, my Velocette, and Bill Bottin's International Norton, as well as all the interested spectators, quite a large contingent by now.

The flying kilometre was the first event, and I returned a time of 26 seconds, equivalent to 86.04 mph. Bill's Norton recorded only 66 mph. He was disgusted with his Certificate and tore it up. The Velo, as I have already stated, returned 79.32 mph to finish 4th. It was the Outer Circuit event that day that was the highlight of the meeting, and unbeknown to me, it was going to have a greater effect on my racing career than any other race in which I had entered. In the Paddock before it started, a figure vaulted over the rails and into my stall. 'I'm from the Ariel works,' he began, 'I see you've got a bit of a non-standard job here. You'd better fit this before you get out onto that Outer Circuit', and he handed me a new Lodge BR 47 plug. He needn't have worried, I already had a BR 49 installed in the head. Anyway, he had a look round, asked if I was alright, and as I answered in the affirmative, he departed. Now Ariels had been plugging their new Red Hunter model rather heavily in the motorcycle press since its introduction, claiming high speed and suitability for trials riding. A large crowd always came on Clubman's Day to see how ordinary riders on every day machines fared, and of course, any make could get a good or a bad name relative to the performance that the crowd saw with their own eyes. A good performance today would be much better than a whole lot of press advertising.

The popularity of Clubman's Day had increased as the following figures prove. The first meeting of 1932 attracted 194 entries which increased to 276 for 1933. By 1934 it had risen to 312, and for this year of grace the number reached 598 entries, the highest number I have been able to trace for any motorcycle race meeting at Brooklands. The crowds had also increased pro rata.

The two fifties and three fifties ran together, the former with 24 seconds start. H.W. Antell, 348 cc Velocette won at 84.41 mph.

All ready for Clubman's Day on 6th April 1935. Bill Bottin's 'International' Norton and the Author's second Ariel, the 1935 single port Red Hunter

THE MOTOR CYCLE

CLUBMAN'S MEETING

This is to Certify that

Mr. A.C. Perryman

at Brooklands Apr. 6th 1935

riding a *497* c.c. *Ariel*

covered

The Flying Kilometre

in _ min. *26* sec., a speed of

86·04 m.p.h.

 Clerk of the Course.

Another Brooklands Certificate, this one relating to the larger capacity Ariel and therefore recording a better time and speed

57

The over 350's had to be run in two heats; the first with 45 riders and the second with 44. Heat one was won by Frank Williams on his not so young 498 cc Cotton Blackburne. This was the occasion on which announcer Graham Walker referred rudely to it as 'the village fire engine', a name that was to remain with it for evermore. It won by 300 yards from J.E. Swaine's 996 cc Brough Superior JAP, and third was H.F. Grinstead, 490 cc Norton.

Heat two, my heat, contained Frank's brother Leonard, and his 498 cc Scott. As soon as the flag fell, Leonard dug at his kickstarter. The Scott fired immediately and was off in a flash. I push started, and by the time I had covered my usual 3 machine lengths and jumped aboard, Leonard was fast receding into the distance. He won at 87.38 mph. I brought the Ariel into second place after a fine scrap with the winner of the previous year's Clubman's Grand Prix, R.D. Spreadbrow, on a 490 cc Manx Norton.

Frank had won his heat at 86.77 mph. So the final placings were (1) L.C. Williams on his Scott, (2) Frank Williams on his Cotton, (3) A.C. Perryman, 497 cc Ariel, (4) R.D. Spreadbrow, Norton, then the Brough and Norton from Heat 1.

It is interesting to record the kilometre speeds of the winners. Swaine's Brough recorded no less than 96.42 mph so he obviously had handling problems around the banked bends. Leonard's Scott clocked 95.60 mph, and was the fastest 500 by 3 1/2 mph. Frank clocked 88.07 mph to finish fifth. I was eighth at 86.04 mph. There was a stiff headwind along the Railway Straight whence the kilometre was situated, and as I had lapped at 91 mph in this race, the Ariel was obviously much faster over the other side of the course. This would also apply to the Scott, which I should think bettered 100 mph on the faster side.

Besides my own Ariel there were about ten other Red Hunters, and the rest of the field made up the fifty seven varieties associated with Club members. The latter followed us home, leaving the aforementioned Hunters to bring up the rear in a solid bunch.

I cannot account for this state of affairs. All I can tell you is that when racing was over for the day, just as we were about to load up, a trilby hatted man came up to shake hands with me, nearly wrenching my arm off in the process. 'My boy' he went on, 'Thank God you were up here today. You've certainly saved our name. Had it not been for you, my life would not have been worth living.' It turned out to be J.R. Darke, the Ariel Sales Representative. All his friends were jeering at him over the performance of his wares. His defence was 'But they **will** go. There was one right out up front, getting the better of a Manx Norton. As for the others, well, it must be the riders'. And he relayed the whole sorry story to me, about the bunch at the rear. I told him that earlier on someone from the works had lent me a plug, should I return it to him. 'That would have been Jack Hunt' he said. (Jack Hunt at that time was Head of the Experimental Department.) 'No, No, Keep it my boy'. He gave me his card and said, 'If there's ever anything you want, write to me at the works, and I'll see that you get it.' With that he shook hands once more and vanished.

The over 350 cc Round the Mountain event had attracted more than 80 entries, who had to perform in three heats. In the first heat, Bill Bottin provided the thrills by diving down the banking to collide with J.R. Bryan on a 499 cc Rudge. For a moment they appeared to be locked together, then they separated safely, waved to each other and carried on. R.H. Newman's 596 cc Scott, won the race at 60.52 mph, followed by C.W.P. Cazenove's 490 cc Norton, and E.A. Beckham, on another 596 cc Scott, was third.

I was in the second heat which E.J. Lemon, on a very rapid 498 Excelsior JAP, won at the highest speed of the day - 63.63 mph. Even so, I managed to steer the Ariel into second place; C.D. Foord on a 490 cc Norton came third. Leonard Williams was in heat three, and there was no holding the Scott, which romped home at 62.31 mph from W.G. Richardson's 490 cc Norton, and W.J.O. Scott's 498 cc Matchless. As the final placings were decided on time, Lemon was the winner, with L.C. Williams second. I was pleased to be in third place with the Ariel, then Newman, Cazenove, and Foord sixth.

There was also a team race at this meeting. Each team had 3 riders. No 1 covered a single Mountain lap, stopped, handed his machine to his pusher-off, ran back to No 2, gave the latter his sash; whereupon No 2 had to repeat the procedure and finally No 3.

Sidcup won the first heat, and the British Two Stroke Club's No. 2 team the second. On times, Sidcup won the final, with their 1st heat runners up; British Two Stroke's No. 1 team was second. The Two Stroke Club's No. 2 team tied for third place with my own club, the Brighton & District MCC;

The start of the Clubman's Senior Mountain Championship on 27th July 1935. The Author (2), is riding his 497 cc Ariel ▷

Rounding the fork hairpin. The Author leads Frank Williams and his 498 cc Cotton Blackburne on 27th July 1935 ▽

KA 781. The 1935 497 cc single port Red Hunter Ariel after it had won the Clubman's Senior Mountain Championship on 27th July 1935

Berkhampstead and the Sunbeam MCC tied for fifth place.

How my own club's team was selected, presumably by the organisers, is rather a mystery. It is given in the list of entries as follows: W.J. Brazier (Royal Enfield) whose name does not appear in the list of entries for any other event, J. Henry (AJS) who had entered under his own club of Worthing Eagle MC in all other events, and Bill Bottin on his Norton, a genuine Brighton rider. I am entered as reserve on my 348 cc Velocette, which was hors de combat with a bent valve after the kilometre trials. How I was not in the team with the Ariel, by far the fastest Brighton machine, and the most experienced of their riders, is not disclosed! There can be no doubt that the two second places in the heats and two thirds in the finals with the Ariel was a fine advertisement for the firm.

I could see that this would be a fine chance for me to turn the Ariel into a pukka racer. I wrote to Mr. Darke, asking if I could have a bronze-cylinder head, like the one I had seen on Ben Bickell's mount. Soon after, I had a letter from Edward Turner, Ariel's Technical Director and Designer. He congratulated me on my performance, and said that he was arranging for a bronze head to be sent to me, and also a special cam which he wanted me to try. He had also fixed up with the Service Department for me to be supplied with any spares I required, for my own use, at a very, very special price. I took the opportunity to renew the exhaust and inlet valves and springs, and also to acquire a BTH racing magneto, to supersede my present Lucas Magdyno.

For 1935 Bemsee had laid on Clubman's Senior and Junior Mountain Championships, to take place on the same day as the regular members meeting on 27th July 1935. I worked on the Ariel's power plant for this, and fitted the new head and cam, plus the racing magneto newly acquired from Selly Oak. I also replaced the standard silencer with a proper Brooklands can.

There was a good field for the Senior Race, 20 starters, including the inevitable Frank Williams with the red painted Cotton Blackburne already christened the 'village fire engine'. I had always had to be content with the rear view of this particular machine, but things were going to be different today. On the fall of the flag the Ariel went straight into the lead and stayed there. Early on there was a chap on a TT Rudge, I believe his name was L.E. Tooth, who came alongside as I neared the turn up on to the Member's Banking. I shut off and took up my line for the corner, but he made no attempt to do likewise. As I swept round on my correct line I could see him out of the corner of my eye, and he appeared to be going straight up the banking. Whether he went over the top or not I never knew, but I never saw him again. Frank had to be content with a rear view of my Ariel this time, *The Motor Cycling* reporting that 'the Senior Event resulted in a runaway win for A.C. Perryman, 497 cc Ariel, who rode splendidly throughout.' I have already reported in a previous chapter what happened to the Velo in the Junior Race. Incidentally, the Velo carried number 1 and finished second. The Ariel carried the number 2 and finished first! The winner's speed in the Senior Race was 64.1 mph. Second was L. Good on a 499 cc Rudge, and third W.J.O. Scott, on a 498 cc Matchless. I returned home in jubilant mood, although a trifle disappointed with the Junior result, but it was my most successful day ever at Brooklands.

Fired by this success, I decided to get an alcohol piston for the grass tracks and the Gatwick Speed

The Author with his 497 cc Ariel after winning the Clubman's Senior Mountain Championship on 27th July 1935 *(Motor Cycle)*

The Clubman's Senior GP held on 18th July 1936. The 43 starters get away. Frank Williams 498 cc Cotton Blackburne (78), W.H. Richardson 490 cc Norton (67), the winner. The Author, 497 cc Ariel (63), led for six laps until forced to drop back with clutch slip *(Motor Cycle)*

Trials. The works could not help in this, so I obtained a Martlett piston from the Brooklands Engineering Co. A double float chamber was also obtained, to feed sufficient fuel which the much larger jets would need. For petrol/benzol mixture I used a 425 jet, and at first on RD1, a 960 jet. Later on I changed over to racing ethyl (Esso) and the jet size required for this was 1500. In this guise I had a go on our local grass track. After my win at Brooklands, I decided that I had finished with trials - it would be racing only from now on. Even so, the large number of points that I gained in my first three trials early in the season, was sufficient to make me the trials champion in the local Brighton & District MCC for 1935.

The Gatwick Speed Trials are covered later on, in a separate chapter, for all my machines.

Unfortunately I did not, in those days, keep a record book. When I did start in 1936, I'm afraid the records are rather meagre and incomplete. However, to return to the grass. At first, I got better results with the Velocette, as it proved lighter on the sharp corners. Later on, after Ariels had sent along a dirt track front wheel and tyre, and I had improved the alcohol performance, it proved its worth and ultimately established the lap record at the local track.

For the Pendennis Road Races on August Bank Holiday, I decided to take the Ariel only, and use the facilities of the Southern Railway Company. I was still employed at the Brighton works, and we were entitled to one free pass each year to anywhere on the parent system. I applied for one from Brighton to Plymouth, and put in for a privilege ticket (quarter fare) from Plymouth to Falmouth on the GWR. There was a through train from Brighton that left about 11.30 am, and according to the timetable I should have been in Falmouth by 8.00 pm. The club secretary had fixed me up with accomodation in the town, and with a large suitcase containing my leathers amongst other clothes, I left the Ariel to the mercy of the guard in his van on that fateful Saturday of 3rd August. The train left on time and was most lethargic in its progress. I hadn't bargained for Navy Week at Portsmouth. It seemed as if there were special trains from the four corners of the earth, all converging on Portsmouth. We had to wait outside until they were all cleared, and so the train was more than an hour late by the time we cleared Portsmouth.

Delays continued all along the line, so that I had not even reached Plymouth by the time I was due in Falmouth. Here I transferred to the GWR and at last progress became faster, Truro being reached as the shades of night were falling. Here I had to change and take the branch line for Falmouth, and for the best part of the next hour, I was engaged in a fine old game of hide and seek to satisfy the playful whims of the two members of the staff on duty.

They assured me that the branch train would leave from the platform where I had disembarked and I was now guarding my precious cycle and suitcase, seated on this same platform. Presently one burst out of the staff room and bawled out 'Passengers for Falmouth over the bridge and take the other platform.' There was an immediate stampede of humanity of all shapes and sizes, complete with their holiday luggage. I looked at that lattice footbridge with its open wooden staircase, and back at the Ariel. No thanks thought I. I consulted the young man who had given the order. 'Best thing t'do mate t'd be t' goo darn end of platform and up t'other side.' I balanced the suitcase on the saddle and struggled across the track, wearily sitting down on a convenient seat as soon as I could. After about ten minutes the second member of the staff appeared, and again 'Passengers for Falmouth, over the bridge and onto the other platform.' rang out. The same mad panic was enacted once more but this time in reverse. I repeated my performance and resumed my previous position on a hard wooden bench.

Sure enough after another ten minutes the door opened once more to give a repeat performance. I decided to bide my time and I was joined by a fellow traveller who had obviously made this trip before. 'Stay where you are friend' he advised. 'They don't know which platform it's coming in on any more than you do. Even when it does arrive there'll be plenty of time. They always pinch the engine off this train to go over the far side of the yard and pick up a couple of vans to tack on the back.' In company with several others I took his advice, whilst an elderly and portly gent informed the miscreants that he would report them to their station master next day.

Well, the train duly arrived, luckily at the platform which I occupied, and sure enough the engine trundled off down the yard. By the time I had stowed the Ariel aboard the guard's van, the rest of the assorted humanity had crowded into all the compartments, which appeared now to be bulging at the seams. The engine returned and resumed its rightful position. I was still pacing the platform, with

The British Motor-Cycle Racing Club

(AFFILIATED TO THE AUTO-CYCLE UNION AS A NON-TERRITORIAL CLUB).

President: Sir Algernon Guinness, Bart.

Chairman of Committee:
Mr. A. V. Ebblewhite.

Hon. Secretary:
J. D. Ferguson.

TELEPHONE: CITY 1067-8

86, Queen Victoria Street,
London, E.C. 4.

D/71711   17th November, 1936.

Dear Perryman,

    Thanks for your letter and postal order value
8/- to cover cost of Dinner Ticket, which I enclose herewith.

    Your speeds in Event 3, when you achieved your
Gold Star were:

        85.87 m.p.h.
      102.06 m.p.h.
       98.82 m.p.h.

    All the best.

          Yours sincerely,

A.C. Perryman, Esq.,
   "The Bakery",
   Old Shoreham,
   Sussex.

A precious piece of paper. This letter confirms the acquisition of a coveted Gold Star, realising the Author's most cherished ambition

A Beamish Brothers advertisement listing some of the achievements of the machines they prepared during the 1937 season

WORTHING EAGLE SCRAMBLE,
April 11th, 1937   (on this Track).

1st

600 c.c. Class— Mr. J. Shenston—*348 c.c. Velocette

350 c.c. Class— Mr. J. Shenston—*348 c.c. Velocette

250 c.c. Class - W. R. Beamish—
                      246 c.c. New Imperial

Handicap—Mr. J. Shenston—*348 c.c. Velocette

Team Race— Messrs.
        J. Shenston, E. Coward, A. C. Perryman

2nd

600 c.c. Class — A. C. Perryman—*497 c.c. Ariel

3rd

350 c.c. Class — E. Coward—346 c.c. New Imperial

All the above machines were
supplied and **TUNED** by

BEAMISH BROS. (Cycles) Ltd.
123, Gardner Road,

Phone—Southwick 9315.   **PORTSLADE.**

Deal with the Experts—THEY KNOW.

* These machines have lapped Brooklands at
    over 102 m.p.h.

4.40 p.m.   **B.M.C.R.C. Members'**   **Event 8 Heat 2**
FIVE-LAP ROUND-THE-MOUNTAIN ALL-COMERS' HANDICAP RACE
Solo Motor Cycles, Motor Cycles exceeding 245 c.c. with Sidecar, and Three Wheelers

No.	Entrant and Driver.	Machine.	Cyls.	Dimensions B.	S.	C.C.	Start M.	S.	No.
2	Pope, N. B.	Norton	1	79 × 100		490	0	0	2
4	Rothwell, Myles (Beart, F. L.)	Norton	1	79 × 100		490	0	3	4
6	Mortimer, C. K.	Norton	1	79 × 100		490	0	8	6
8	Waite, J. B.	Norton	1	79 × 100		490	0	11	8
10	Brooks, C. M.	Norton	1	79 × 100		490	0	11	10
12	Talbot-Ponsonby, E. F.	Norton	1	79 × 100		490	0	16	12
14	Sandison, J.	Norton	1	79 × 100		490	0	16	14
16	Webster, G. W.	Vincent H.R.D.	1	84 × 90		499	0	16	16
18	Gargano, D. A. L.	Norton	1	79 × 100		490	0	16	18
20	Perryman, A. C.	Ariel	1	81.8 × 95		497	0	16	20
22	Mobbs, E. G.	Velocette	1	74 × 81		348	0	23	22
24	Whitworth, M. D.	Triumph	1	84 × 89		497	0	26	24
26	Lunn, W. R.	Velocette	1	74 × 81		348	0	30	26
28	Fry, F. W.	Velocette	1	74 × 81		348	0	30	28
30	Lamacraft, H. C.	Velocette	1	74 × 81		348	0	30	30
32	Milward, H. K.	Velocette	1	74 × 81		348	0	30	32
34	Smith, G. H. A.	Velocette	1	74 × 81		348	0	30	34
36	Tooth, L. E.	Rudge	1	70 × 90		349	0	30	36
38	Allen, C. D.	Excelsior	1	62.5 × 80		247	0	36	38
40	Gatley, C. M.	Chater-Lea	1	71 × 88		348	0	36	40
42	Board, R.	Excelsior	1	67 × 70		250	0	43	42

RESULT: First 20 Second 22 Third 8 Fourth 30 Fifth 30 Sixth 2

WINNER'S SPEED: 67.61 m.p.h. Time: ....mins. ....secs.

FINAL PLACINGS: First 20 Second 22 Third 8 Fourth 30 Fifth 23 Sixth 2

A page from Motor Cycle's Clubman's Day meeting at Brooklands on 17th April 1937. It was in the Five-Lap Round-The-Mountain All-Comers Handicap Race that the Author put in an outstanding performance

suitcase, seeking a place. The guard looked at me with a kindly smile. 'We're just going mate. You'd better come in with me, if you want to get there tonight; this is the last train.' So I piled into his van and flopped wearily down on the Ariel's welcome saddle. It was now around midnight, so as soon as the train had reduced to a crawl in Falmouth station I leapt out and sprinted outside to accost the only taxi in the place. I told the driver where I wanted to go, but couldn't leave then as I had the Ariel to house on the station for the night. Just then the rest of the horde disgorged from the station, many piling into the taxi. The driver grinned at me, 'Don't worry guv'nor. I'll be back for you when I've seen this lot orf. Jest you sit there and wait for me, don't go away.' He needn't have added the last words. The place was all darkness outside and I hadn't a clue as to which direction to take to reach my goal that night. I returned to the station, just in time to rescue the Ariel as the train was to back out into the yard for the night. The one remaining porter I found very co-operative, and he unlocked the Left Luggage Department into which I bundled the Ariel for the night. I sat down on my case outside to await the taxi, the porter having locked up, turned off the lights and departed. I had not quite dropped off to sleep by the time my faithful friend turned up with his taxi, and he took me along to the house I named. The good lady had gone to bed, having given me up some time ago. However, she sympathised with me over my misfortunes, and I squared up with the taxi driver and thanked him. After a good wash and a bedtime cuppa, I was soon sound asleep. The time was almost 1.30 am. The station being right on the course, I left the Ariel there until the morning of the race, then removed it and pushed it along into the Paddock.

The race itself proved rather an anti-climax for me. I could enter only the 500 cc race of course, and George Rowley was present with a works AJS; needless to relate, he won. The Ariel was still fitted with its original cork-plated clutch, and this took exception to the many gear changes and rapid acceleration that this course demanded. Before it finally burnt out I had the satisfaction of making the fastest lap by a member of the promoting club. Had the Ariel behaved itself, I would most likely have been second to George, as the bike circulated very rapidly whilst the clutch held out. After the racing was over, I pushed the Ariel back to the station for the night, collected it on the Tuesday morning and came home in disgust. The journey this time was quite straightforward, and passed off without incident.

The oil-bath chaincase had been retained for the Pendennis event, the last time it was ever used in racing. Upon dismantling it, a most appalling smell of burnt cork filled the workshop and persisted for days. I had recently signed up with Ferodo's to use their brake and clutch linings, and as they had already dealt with the brakes, the clutch plates were hurriedly put in the post to be fitted with their fabric racing linings. I had stressed the urgency of the relining as I was due at the Gatwick Speed Trials in a few days. With creditable efficiency, so lacking nowadays, the plates were back by return of post! Selly Oak had also despatched some much stronger clutch springs for the fabric clutch lining, and a cast aluminium chainguard to replace the original oil bath. This also necessitated the addition of a drip feed oiler for the chain, fed from the original oil gauge feed pipe.

We did not realise in those days how lucky we were to have such an efficient postal service. One had only to write to the Works Service Department, and if you could get the letter in the post by 8.00 pm, the night postal from Euston made sure it was on the office desk in the morning. The Service Department dealt with it the same day, and it would be back the day following, or if a big parcel, a further day later at the worst. I think had we have had to rely on today's methods we probably should have missed quite a few races.

After my runaway win round the Mountain, I thought that I stood a very good chance in the 50 mile Clubman's Grand Prix on 31st August, which would be my last run at Brooklands for 1935. There appeared to be nothing to do to the motor. I could not improve on its last performance, so I checked over all the adjustments and left well alone. Practice was concentrated on the Velo. The Ariel seemed quite happy that day, so I took it back and concentrated on the Velo as that was far from satisfactory.

There were 34 starters and when the flag fell, the Mountain course again prevailed. The Ariel went straight into the lead, and stayed there. It is worth recording that in this Senior race, a solid phalanx of riders converged on the barrels marking the bends in the Finishing Straight, after the leaders had gone through. Realising that this mob could not possibly get through en masse, the marshals fled, and left them to it! Barrels were sent flying in all directions, and the problem then became to dodge the rolling barrels, not to steer a course through them. In *The Motor Cycle* report a photo appeared of this, with the caption 'The rider who appears to have a steam roller's front wheel, is D.W. Ronan, 499 cc Rudge. This

Winning the Unlimited class, Sompting grass track, 1937 ▷

◁ The most successful Clubman's Day of 17th April 1937. 1st in the 5th lap event, 3rd in the 10 laps Round the Mountain; left to right, Norman Cox, the Author, Jack Piper, Mrs. Lil Riley, Jim Riley and the 497 cc Ariel

Sompting grass track June 1937. J. Shenston, 348 cc Velocette (15), nearly rams the Author's 497 cc Ariel (67) at the foot of the 1 in 4 hill in the 600 cc race. The Ariel finished first ▷

was in the BMCRC member's race for 1934.

By the time I had arrived for my second passage, most of the barrels had been reinstated, only to be scattered again when the bunch arrived almost as densely packed as before. I completed three laps in the lead and saw no one. Coming off the Byfleet Banking on lap 4 I could feel the motor tighten up and I whipped out the clutch. I coasted in, and pushed the rest to the pits. Everyone, of course, went by. My Mountain victory was not going to be repeated, as the motor had gone solid. A subsequent strip down when we got home luckily revealed no serious damage. The piston had run dry at the back, and picked up. At the end of the season I decided to take an oil lead direct to the back of the cylinder base. After this I had no more trouble. Anyway that was the finish of racing for the day. I had to be content with my second in the Junior Race, as already reported. The result was first C. Bayly, 499 cc Rudge, 75.04 mph, second W.C. Watkins 490 cc Norton, and third W.G. Richardson, also on a 490 cc Norton.

The Ariel had certainly proved itself, and I hoped to cure its teething troubles during the winter to make 1936 even better.

The first blow in 1936 was not being able to compete on Clubman's Day, as already reported. So, it was grass track and Gatwick until the Grand Prix came round again, the restrictive clause having been dispensed with. Practice passed off well enough, no snags being apparent. I have already recounted the fracas of the extra lap in the Junior, and what with that and still feeling sore at that oiled up plug, I was not in a very good mood when I got back from the Timekeeper's Box. After explaining what happened there, there was little time to get on the Ariel and get to the start. Jack Piper told me that he had checked it over, and found the only thing needing attention was clutch adjustment. He thought the play excessive so had taken it up. Little did he, or I for that matter, know that in so doing he had sealed my fate.

There were so many lined up on the track for this race, 35 in all, that there was no room for Ebby to stand with his flag! So, he stood up on the barrier at the track's edge, steadied by a boy scout who very conveniently happened to be present. Duncan Ferguson, the Secretary, was worried over safety and said 'Give way rather than touch, lads.' The reply to this came from Wally Richardson, the ultimate winner. 'We're only amateurs Mr Ferguson.' With this Ebby dropped his flag and away we went.

Whether we were so densely packed that it distracted me I don't know, but I certainly wasn't first

A spectator's view of Brooklands taken from the Member's Hill on 17th July 1937. An Outer Circuit handicap race is in progress *(Motor Cycle)*

into the corner. Frank Williams and the Cotton had already got there, and so had several others. But once I was round the corner and had settled down along the straight, I passed the others and chased after Frank. Once again the Ariel had the advantage, and I was soon back where I wanted to be, in the lead. I stayed there for about six laps, and then at the end of the Railway Straight, Frank drew alongside, grinning all over his face, and holding his nose! He must have found a bit more I decided, and I tried to tuck myself away more. But it didn't make any difference and he pulled away. On the next lap another rider passed, then another, then two more and I knew by now that something was amiss. As I accelerated away from the barrels, the bike's acceleration did not match that of the motor. The clutch was slipping. As it got hot, of course, it expanded, and eliminated the meagre clearance that Jack had left. I carried on, anything over half throttle producing slip. The race was lost now anyway, whatever I did from now on, so I decided to enjoy the ride as best I could. I did at least finish the race, the power plant sounding as healthy as ever. The clutch did not burn out as it did at Falmouth, but I could not use anything like full potential. The race was won by W.G. Richardson on a 490 cc Manx Norton at 73.39 mph, H.M. Powell brought his 497 cc Ariel into second place, and third was R. Harrison, on a 495 cc AJS. The race was 1.65 mph slower than the last year's, owing to the strong wind.

All in all, a disastrous day. This was to be the very last Clubman's race in which I rode. The powers that be had cried enough. Funnily they didn't seem to mind Frank! He finished sixth in the Round the Mountain scratch race at the next Clubman's day, but by then I was already a Bemsee member and had my most successful day ever at Brooklands with the Ariel. Before that there is the last race of 1936 to report.

Soon after the Grand Prix a letter arrived from Bemsee setting out the position for the future and offering membership of the club. Any subscription paid now would cover membership not only for the rest of 1936 but the whole of 1937 as well. The offer was very tempting and I took the bait! My days as a Clubman were over! Now that I was a regular member my thoughts immediately turned to a Gold Star for a lap at 100 mph or over during a race. The Ariel had lapped at 91 mph on its first appearance in 1935, on petrol. It was a bit faster now, and turned over to alcohol fuel, a 100 mph lap should be possible. I decided to have a try at the October 10th meeting. The award would make a splendid present for my 24th birthday, if I were lucky enough to gain it, albeit a day late! So the two three lap handicaps on the Outer Circuit were entered. If unlucky in the first, then I could try again in the second.

The longest race I had ever done on alcohol up till then was on grass tracks, and that would be very different to three laps of the Outer Circuit, nearly nine miles. With my Martlett piston it was possible to get a compression ratio of 13.75 to 1. This gave a head to piston clearance of about 0.010 in when cold. I only ever used it like this once in my life, at Gatwick's quarter mile the following year. The only thing to better it that day was Noel Pope's supercharged Brough Superior!

I was not fool enough to expect to go round Brooklands with that sort of clearance, and I had fitted a compression plate. Even so the ratio was probably over 12 to 1. My first excursions on alcohol were made on RD1 with a 960 jet, and luckily this was also the first time I entered particulars in a log book. Apart from the use of RD1 fuel, the cycle was just as it had been used on Clubman's Day. No dropped narrow bars or saddle over the rear wheel. Standard handlebars, saddle, and pad on the rear mudguard were the order of the day, and they certainly did **not** enhance the performance.

Practice in the morning revealed the necessary urge, but after a couple of laps an ominous tapping was emanating from the power plant, so I returned to the Paddock to investigate. We could only surmise that the piston was hitting the head, and decided to strip the motor. Sure enough, marks on the piston confirmed this. The problem now was to obtain another compression plate, so a frantic visit to the sheds at the track was the next move. No one wanted to take it on, and after several refusals, at last one kind soul agreed to help. I had the barrel with me, but the only available material was some rather thin aluminium, too thin in fact. So two were manufactured, it was that or nothing, and I settled up and dashed back to the paddock. The motor was hurriedly re-assembled, and the petrol tank refitted. Only just in time; the riders were filing out of the gate to go to the starting line. We hadn't even time to start the motor. I grabbed my helmet and a racing plug, and we just managed to push the bike through the gate before it closed for the last time. The Ariel started alright and I rode it to the line with Jack on the pillion. Here the racing plug was fitted, and I thought out my plan of attack. Would the piston now clear? If not, it would probably disintegrate. To try and do anything in the race would be inadvisable. I

67

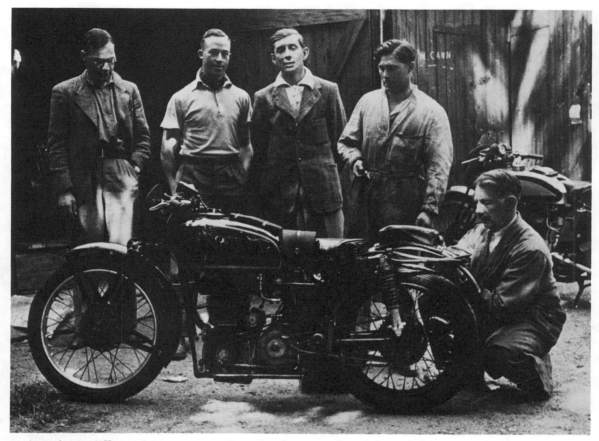

At the Falcon Cliff Hotel Garage, Douglas, Isle of Man. Left to right, unknown, Maurice Cann, Les Archer, Dennis Offord, whilst J.C. (Pa) Archer, makes some adjustments to his 'precious piece of machinery' in the shape of a Senior 495 cc Velocette, ridden by Les at Brooklands in 1937 *(L.J. Archer)*

would take the first lap easy and at three quarter distance open right out for the second lap. If I still had an operative power plant after that I would leave it on for the third lap.

This plan duly worked and I was surprised to reach the Paddock in one piece. A colleague well versed in timing had put his stop watch on me for lap two. He was emphatic that I had done it and gave me a time of 98 seconds, which was within the requisite 99 1/2 seconds maximum. On enquiry of the timekeepers, back came the gloomy news, no Gold Stars in that race.

The Ariel was wheeled out once more for me to have another go in the second race, following the same plan. It was slower this time, and rain was beginning to fall. Actual misfiring occurred on the last lap, and it entered the Paddock, pinking, knocking and sounding decidedly unhappy. We left the track deciding that the settings would need considerable revision for next year. I had finished fifth in the first event, and the next thing was a surprise letter from Secretary, Duncan Ferguson, asking me to attend the annual Dinner to collect my Gold Star! My second lap had been reeled of in 97 seconds, a speed of 102.06 mph. The standing lap amazed me:- 85.87 mph when I was touring until three quarter distance. The third lap was reeled off at 98.88 mph. My tactics had paid off in that first race. In retrospect, Lady Luck certainly rode with me that day! To lap at that speed, at the first attempt on alcohol, with settings that obviously left a lot to be desired, can hardly be described otherwise. I didn't even know the correct compression ratio, but a later measurement with the two compression plates fitted gave 11 to 1.

For 1937 a TT36 light alloy carburettor was acquired, hoping that a more modern instrument might produce a bit more urge. The first event was the local grass track meeting on 11th April. Using a compression ratio of 10 to 1 and RD1 fuel, the best I could manage was a second in the 600 cc class, beaten by Bill Beamish's Velocette, in spite of my dirt track front wheel. I retired in the handicap event, with a broken clutch lever anchorage. Evidently the power plant was not on its best behaviour, as the log

The eighth race of the first road race meeting of 17th July 1937. Dennis Loveday (7) 497 cc Ariel, E.J. Cashman (6) 490 cc Norton, both on 27 sec. mark, J.B. Moss (4) 490 cc Norton, 16 sec. mark, the Author (3) 497 cc Ariel, 10 sec. mark, Ron Harris (1) 490 cc Norton, scratch *(C.G. Griffiths)*

'Ebby' steps back as the Author pushes off in the Ariel's very last race on 17th July 1937 *(C.G. Griffiths)*

The Brooklands Senior GP of 1937. The author (19) on his 497 cc Ariel, has a ding-dong scrap with Maurice Cann, 490 cc Norton, on the Campbell circuit

69

A model B14 498 cc Excelsior JAP ridden by G.R. Stanley during 1936. The Author came near to purchasing one of these machines in 1932 *(Motor Cycle)*

records that three clutch lever anchors broke during the afternoon! The record concludes:- 'Performance **not** up to expectation,' and that was the last time I ever used RD1.

The next event was the 17th April Clubman's Day meeting at Brooklands and here the Ariel gave its best ever performance at the track. I had entered a five lap and a ten lap Round the Mountain Race and can do no better than record extracts from *The Motor Cycle* report on the races. in the five lapper I had 16 seconds start from scratch, and the race was run in two heats. The race report reads:

'Lockett, however, was not to win. Coming up with a wet sail was a very fast Ariel in the hands of D.A. Loveday, who won at 62.77 mph by a mere twenty yards; second was Lockett and third A.J. Lawrance (490 cc Norton).' In Heat two 'an Ariel was again the winner. A.C. Perryman (497 cc Ariel) lay fifth on Lap one, third on lap two, first on lap three and won as he pleased at a speed of 67.61 mph with E.G. Mobbs (348 cc Velocette) second, and J.B. Waite (490 cc Norton) third. The final order, owing to the second heat being easily the faster was this trio, followed by H.C. Lamacraft (348 cc Velocette), D.A. Loveday, and N.B. Pope (490 cc Norton)." I could never understand the wording of this scribe's report, in view of the fact that Dennis's average was nearly 5 mph **slower** than mine!

'Ebby', Mr. A.V. Ebblewhite, watches his timing clocks prior to dropping his Union Jack starter's flag at the start of a 3 lap Outer Circuit Race held on the 23rd May 1936. The next batch of riders are about to be dispatched on their way. The man in the trilby hat and raincoat behind the riders is Duncan Ferguson, BEMSEE Secretary *(Motor Cycle)*

The first road race meeting held on the Campbell Circuit on 17th July 1937. This photograph shows the start of the Junior Road Championship which was won by Harold Daniell (11) on his 348 cc Norton. Les Archer (18) was second on his 348 cc Velocette *(Motor Cycle)*

For my win in this five lapper, I was rehandicapped for the ten laps, being put back from the 31 second mark to 14 seconds; less than I received in the five laps! *The Motor Cycle* reported: Heat one was Lockett's own special race, for he and his Norton led for all ten laps. There was plenty of really fast work however, and this time the scratch men N.B. Pope (490 cc Norton) and R. Harris (490 cc Norton) cut through the field in great style, though Lockett was too much for them. He averaged 65 mph, but the second heat was still faster and the first six in Heat two were the first six in the final placings of the handicap. In Heat two it was also a case of a man leading from lap one to the finish. H.C. Lamacraft (348 cc Velocette) won by 250 yards from A.C. Perryman (497 cc Ariel) at a speed of 66.09 mph, and the final order was Lamacraft, Lockett, Perryman, N.B. Pope (490 Norton), R. Harris and C. Bayly (490 Norton).'

In these two races the limit man had 20 seconds start on me for five laps, and 57 seconds start in the ten lapper, upon my re-handicap. I was very pleased with this result. To have 14 seconds start in ten laps (1.4 seconds per lap) on two such fast scratch men as Noel Pope and Ron Harris and to have come in ahead of them cheered me up no end! I had got the Ariel motoring on alcohol this time, its first run on Esso racing ethyl. The compression ratio is recorded as 11.4 to 1.

The official Brooklands results (available only after the script was compiled) differ from *The Motor Cycle* report. Most likely they were amended when race times were examined in more detail, some time after the results had been announced on the day. The corrected list for Heat two of the ten lap race is:- (1) H.C. Lamacraft (2) J. Lockett 348 cc Norton (3) A.C. Perryman 497 Ariel (4) N.B. Pope 490 Norton (5) R. Harris 490 Norton (6) C. Bayly 490 Norton.

Selly Oak had suggested that a 250 cc fork spring might improve the handling, and one was tried here for the first time. It certainly did! My report ends:- 'Engine perfectly cool and performance more than expected. No trouble at all.'

Incidentally, Dennis Loveday's Ariel was the one that C.B. Bickell showed me, and on which the latter was tragically killed in the Ulster Grand Prix.

Delighted with this Brooklands performance, I decided to use the same settings for the local grass

During the Senior Road Championship of 17th July 1937 J.B. Waite, 490 cc Norton (11), leads J.B. Moss, 490 cc Norton (17), and F.P. Heath, 498 cc Vincent HRD, round the banking bend and out on to the Members Banking. The Clubhouse can be seen in the left background *(Motor Cycle)*

L.J. Archer (20) riding Stanley Woods' 495 cc Velocette prepares to sweep past A.J. Rawlance, 490 cc Norton, as they leave the Test Hill hairpin in the Senior Road Championship of 17th July 1937. Archer finished second with Rawlance sixth *(Motor Cycle)*

A team race between Donington riders (wearing white sashes) and BEMSEE riders (wearing yellow sashes) was held during the first road race meeting of 17th July 1937. L.J. Archer, 348 cc Velocette (12), rides for BEMSEE and chases G.H. Hayden, 348 cc Velocette (4), who represents Donington, into the Test Hill Hairpin. Donington won the event *(Motor Cycle)*

track meeting on 30th May, substituting a cast iron cylinder head for its bronze counterpart. (I used the iron one on grass and the bronze one at Brooklands) and changed the engine sprocket from one of 23 teeth to one of 19 teeth. The compression ratio and carburettor settings remained the same. The Brooklands performance was repeated. My log book records:- 600 cc race first. Team Race first. Handicap race (from scratch) fourth, and concludes 'Engine perfect throughout.'

Bemsee introduced Wednesday afternoon meetings in 1934, and I entered a five lap Mountain race on June 30th. Ebby had now got the measure of the Ariel, and I found myself next to scratch man Ron Harris. I had three seconds start on Ron in five laps and he was on a works Norton. Off we went in fine style, Ron not making an inch on the Ariel. By lap two I had placed a Velocette between myself and Ron. On lap three Ron shot by, followed by the Velocette. I was still circulating, but rather slowly, so I rode into the Paddock, the power plant sounding decidedly unhealthy. Subsequent stripping revealed that the crankpin had sheared across the oil holes.

I entered only one more Mountain event after this and it is not recorded in the book so I can give no details. Evidently I was unplaced, most likely through too severe a handicap. I record it here, as I came within an ace of a very nasty pile up. I was having a fine scrap with Johnny Waite on his 490 cc Manx Norton. The Ariel was perhaps a shade faster but not enough to overhaul him. We swept out of the fork hairpin and really let them have it, Johnny about ten yards ahead. Determined to get by, I lowered my head right down and looked at the petrol tank instead of ahead. He should now be right ahead I thought, time to look up and get by. I looked up; he was right ahead alright, almost under my front wheel and getting nearer very rapidly. I just had time to lean hard left and mercifully scraped by without touching him, but it was very, very close. Back in the Paddock I asked him what happened. 'The plug lead jumped off' Johnny grinned in reply. 'Yes, and we both very nearly emanated it' I told him, 'Through my stupidity'. I never took my eyes off the track after that, however much I wanted more speed!

The next meeting was on the Campbell Circuit (road race) on 17th July and this, of course, was on petrol-benzole. I was less successful on this fuel. Whereas I could hold all but the **very** fastest Nortons on alcohol, it was a very different story on petrol.

For this first meeting Ebby the Handicapper paid me a fine compliment, evidently from my Mountain performance in April. The Ariel was No 3, and had fifteen seconds start over the two scratch men, Noel Pope and Maurice Cann, both on hot 490 cc Nortons. Even my friend Johnny Waite was allowed nine seconds start on me! The race was a gift for the early starters. G.H. Hayden won on his Velocette, and Dave Whitworth was second on his 250 cc Cotton.

The second long handicap (five laps) was a repeat performance. I was No 2 this time, again with fifteen seconds start on scratch man Ron Harris. Johnny Waite once more had a nine seconds start on me. Again the 350 Velocettes, with starts of 1 minute 43 seconds and 1 minute 21 seconds were too much for the back markers, and they took four of the first 5 places. F.W. Fry won and J. Moore was second on his 490 cc Norton, Basil Keys managed a fifth place with his Velo. Even Donington Star J.B. Moss was given nine seconds start on me!

I was also in the second short handicap (three laps) No 2 again, and with ten seconds start on scratch man, Dave Whitworth, this time on a 494 cc Triumph. Now it was the 250's turn, and F.N. Pearce won on his New Imperial from L.A. Dear, on another 250 New Imp, off the 1 minute 11 seconds mark. A 350 cc Velocette was third.

I'm afraid the Ariel did not justify Ebby's assessment of its potential, and I was unable to get any-where near the early starters.

An innovation at this first meeting was a match race between Bemsee and Donington teams of five riders each. I was surprised and delighted to see my name, and also that of Dennis Loveday, in the list of eleven riders from which the selections were to be made. In the event our Ariels were not called upon to uphold the Bemsee name, and Donington won, Noel Pope being first and Maurice Cann second. A.J. Rawlence and Johnny Waite had to be content with fifth and sixth places for Bemsee on their Nortons.

The Senior Road Championship attracted twenty three riders, who were dispatched in a massed start, with no handicaps. It demonstrated in no uncertain fashion the advantage to be gained from a rapid start.

74

L.J. Archer had a pukka works 500 cc Velocette with square fins and rear wheel springing.

Enthusiasts were poring over this with envious eyes, whilst Pa Archer stood around to see that no one meddled with this precious piece of machinery.

We were in batches of three on the grid and Les was alongside me. On the petrol tank he had fastened a sheet of paper emblazoned with the legend 'Down for up, and up for down'. Several riders were amused by this, and one asked Les, 'What's the matter, don't you know how to manage the bloody thing?' Les replied 'This is Stanley Wood's patent, and it's the opposite way round to my bike.' It looked a most formidable opponent, with its huge tank and cylinder head, and of course, it had a high bottom gear for the Isle of Man course. My Ariel had a lower bottom gear than any of the IOM type, which made up the bulk of the entry, and when the flag fell, a few paces and bump! I was into the saddle and away before any of the others fired. The acceleration was superb, and I was coming out of the Test Hill Hairpin, as the first bend had been named, as the others were still struggling with their high bottom gears.

H.L. Daniell's Norton was much faster than any other of the same marque, but he was only sixth into that hairpin, whilst Les was nearly last. So great was the advantage gained by that start that I was first through on that first lap and going down the Railway Straight on my second, having just attained maximum speed, when Harold shot by on that Norton, about 25 mph faster. He then proceeded to establish a colossal lead, setting a new lap record at 68.35 mph, and winning the race at 67.04 mph.

No one else came by on that lap, but on the next Noel Pope came by, although not as fast as Harold. Then Maurice Cann appeared and he and I had a fine scrap for a little while. But these Nortons were too much for me on petrol fuel, and I was losing ground every lap. About lap six, Les hurtled past me down the straight, if anything going even faster than Harold, with a lap at 68.12 mph. The Velocette had taken several laps to get really motoring, and was now making up for lost time. Les eventually finished second, but was unable to make up all the ground he had lost to Harold in the early stages. Noel Pope was third, Jock Forbes fourth and Maurice Cann fifth, all on Nortons.

The pace had been hot, and about half the entry had retired. I finished the ten laps, about twenty two and a half miles, well down the field!

Chapter Six
Excelsior

It happened this way. I had left the Brighton railway works to take up a position with a firm of car repairers (garage otherwise!). Tom Fassett, who had supplied my first Ariel, was the Works Foreman there, after his motorcycle business had folded up. I had been there only a few weeks when Bill Beamish asked me if I would like to go and work for him, with a view to eventual partnership. I jumped at this chance; it was cycles and motorcycles only, and we were both keen on racing as much as possible. I joined Bill in the summer of 1936, when he was agent for Rudge, BSA, and New Imperial.

After my Brooklands successes, I contacted Ariel Motors, and we were soon agents for them as well. Anyone locally interested in racing was certain, sooner or later, to visit us, as there were always racing machines about the place. I have already related the tale of the local builder, Ernie, and in 1937 history repeated itself with another local builder; this time I will identify him as 'Peter' although that wasn't his real name. Peter wanted a pukka racer, and aiming higher than Ernie, he fancied a crack at the Isle of Man.

Now Bill had twice competed there, in 1931 on a Senior Rudge and 1936 on a 250 cc New Imperial, both times in the Manx Grand Prix. He advised Peter it would be best to have a 250, a newcomer would find that easier than a modern 500. The outcome was that Peter ordered a 250 Excelsior Manxman, if Bill could get it. The firm agreed to supply one, and promised delivery in time for the Manx Grand Prix.

Every now and then Peter would arrive with the usual female escorts to see if it had arrived. After impressing his escorts with what he was about to do in the Isle of Man he would take his leave. There was still no sign of the 250, and frantic calls to the works only evoked the promise that it would be ready in time for the Manx.

Peter arrived one day on his own. Where was it? We didn't know. Bill got worried. Entries had already closed at single fees. Then Peter came right out with it. He had got cold feet! Would I ride it for him, if he sent in the entry? Bill had already entered Jack Shenston on his 250 New Imperial and suggested that I went along as well and we'd make it our holiday. Peter paid the late entry double fee, and a few days before we were due to leave for the Isle of Man, we still hadn't got the Excelsior. We were then told to call at the works and collect it en route for the Island.

Bill's car was an old six cylinder Rover Sportsmans Coupe which he had purchased from the local car wrecker for £5. We hitched to it our home-made trailer, which carried two machines. The Rover had an unholy thirst for oil, and a special 5 gall drum of the cheapest brand we could buy was kept especially for it. On setting out we topped up the sump, and then took the remains of the drum's contents with us in a 1 gallon can. So prodigious was the Rover's appetite for the stuff that we were having to purchase oil from Oxford onwards! We arrived at the Excelsior works only to be told that the machine still wasn't ready, and that Alan Bruce and Ginger Wood would deliver it to us in the Island, along with the ones required by others for the race.

When we arrived on the quay at Liverpool, we unloaded the New Imp. and the gear, and loaded it aboard the steamer. 'What shall we do with the Rover, Bill?' I asked. 'Leave the bloody thing where it is'

In the Paddock at Brooklands 1938. The Author is now on his 248 cc Excelsior Manxman ⇨

⇦ Cunningham's Camp during September 1937. The Author (248 cc Excelsior) with pit attendant J. McDonnell, extreme right

The Author, 248 cc Excelsior Manxman, waiting to start the 1937 Manx GP. He was the last rider to retire, lying sixth with eight miles to go *(C.G. Griffiths)* ⇨

he retorted, 'Nobody will pinch **that**'. 'What about the trailer?'. 'Same goes for that' came the reply. The landing in the Island went off smoothly, and we all booked in at Cunningham's Holiday Camp, near Douglas.

Practice started on the Thursday morning. I had no mount, but went along with the others to watch the fun. We kept a watching brief on the steamer arrivals, and at last on the Saturday, the Excelsior arrived! Alan Bruce instructed me on what had and what had **not** to be done, and said that after practice, it had to be taken along to their hotel, where the works mechanics would have it down and prepare it for race day.

My first run on it was the Monday, and I had an easy lap on wet roads to get used to it and the course. I managed a 2nd lap before the road was re-opened. Jack Shenstone meanwhile, with his usual tactics, had shown no mercy to the New Imp, and had put the connecting rod through the crankcase!

On the second morning, I foolishly decided to go round on the warming-up plug as I was only touring. After the ascent of Creg Willeys Hill, the soft plug cried enough, and misfiring began. I eased right off to try and coax the bike back to the start. I had not considered the climb up the Mountain! As things turned out, I didn't have to. Reaching the Sulby Straight I realised that everyone would be going much faster than me round the right hander over the bridge, and was not looking forward to being rammed from the rear. I decided to get right over on the left and then make a sharp turn on the bridge, to keep out of everyone else's cornering line. I must have been proceeding faster than I thought, and when I got in some loose gravel on the bridge, the rear wheel slid in this and down we went. I slid along on my backside and my left foot came into violent contact with the bridge parapet. The cycle turned right round, and the top of the rear mudguard also hit the parapet, pushing it down on to the tyre.

The transport that collected lame ducks came to the rescue, and I returned to the start by that means. I had turned my ankle over, and by the time Douglas was reached it was very swollen and I could hardly walk. Back at the camp I had to spend the next two days on my bed, to keep weight off it, and the doctor visited me regularly.

Jack, in the meantime, could not practice, in view of the well ventilated crankcase, so Bill suggested he should borrow the Excelsior to learn the course. 'For God sake don't let him blow that up as well' I pleaded. 'Don't worry' said Bill, 'I've read the riot act to him, and he's going to take it steady.' 'That'll be the day when **he** takes it steady' I retorted, but as I was immobile I could not prevent the Excelsior being used for Jack's practicing. Mercifully, the New Imperial factory despatched another engine lower half by air, and the cycle was rendered operative once more before he could damage the Excelsior.

With practice nearly over, the doctor relented and said I could resume practice, but not to do much walking about, to give it a chance to heal.

'Righto' said Bill, 'In the morning, up bright and early, and get out and put in two laps, three if you can.'

The chalet next to ours was occupied by other racers, including Tommy Wood, making his first appearance on a Velocette. We decided to turn in early to be able to get up early in the morning.

Tommy had other ideas, and made as much noise as he could, shouting obscenities across the top of the intervening partition, which kept us awake. As it got darker he produced a petrol blow lamp, and pumped it up, squirting a jet of petrol into our chalet. This was too much for Bill. 'Bloody fool' he bellowed, 'If I'd been smoking you'd have blown the lot of us up'. I think even Tommy realised the folly of his pranks now, and that seemed to terminate them.

However, also attached to the camp was Tommy McEwan, who was to ride Junior and Senior Nortons, and a few colleagues from North of the border. We had managed to get to sleep after the earlier episode when there was quite a commotion outside as Tommy and his mates returned from a late drinking session. Evidently, they had got mixed up with the night watchman, who was on his rounds. We were all semi-conscious, and Bill evidently thought it time to rise. 'Better get up and get down the start' he called out to me. 'Yes alright' I replied drowsily, but I must have dropped off again, as the next thing I knew Bill was in a rage and bawling out at me 'Come on Bert, get out of there and get started'. I wearily turned out of bed and got dressed, putting my leathers on, boots and all. I opened the door; my! was it dark outside.

I made my way slowly to the big garage reserved for the Manx entrants, and slid back the glass door, then switched on the light. The Excelsior was near the the door, so I pushed it outside, turned off

Jack Shenstone, 246 cc New Imperial, awaits starter's orders in the 1937 Manx GP. He was the first rider to retire *(C.G. Griffiths)*

Manx GP September 1937. The Author, 248 cc Excelsior (25), about to pass A. Fox, 248 cc Excelsior (6), near Signpost Corner *(Motor Cycling)*

The author gets well down to it
on his 248 cc Excelsior, passing
the start on the Campbell
Circuit. 14th May 1938

The Author, 248 cc Excelsior ready to
start in a handicap race on the
Campbell Circuit in 1938. Basil Keys
is to the rear of the left handlebar.
R.R.C. Palmer, 248 cc Excelsior
alongside, adjusts his goggles
(C.G. Griffiths)

Ron Harris, 490 cc Norton (1), about to pass the Author, 248 cc Excelsior (22), the limit man, on the
Campbell Circuit 14th May 1938 *(Motor Cycle)*

the lights, and shut the door. It must be very early I thought, it's so dark. Better not start up till I'm out in the road, so I started to push.

The beam from a torch shone out and illuminated both rider and cycle. 'And where do you think you're going then' a voice asked of me. It was the night watchman. 'Why, out to practice' I replied angrily. 'What, at half past two in the morning?' the watchman queried. 'Is that all it is' I asked. 'That's it' he said, 'Better get back to bed for a couple of hours!'. I thanked my lucky stars that I had not started the motor, for it would have awoken the whole camp. I would probably have been expelled. By the time I'd returned and got back to sleep, it was almost time to start all over again. Anyhow, I did get out, and put in a couple of good laps, although there was no time for a third.

The practicing over, the machine was taken along to the hotel garage where the Excelsior works people stayed and turned over to Ginger Wood; there were quite a few Excelsiors to be dealt with, and he told me to return about a day later to collect it.

On the eve of the race a few of us decided to go out for a drink, and in the bar of a local hostelry we met Ginger. He was trying to pacify one of the riders, living in fear of what might befall him in the race. 'Don't worry about it' said Ginger, 'When your time has come, whether you're lying in bed, or lapping the Island, you'll go, but not before. Take me for instance. I came off the New Imperial big twin in the Hutchy at nearly 120 mph, and only sprained my thumb. Attending the local doctor's surgery I came across a chap with his arm in a sling and bits of sticky plaster on his face. 'Whatever happened to you?' Ginger asked. 'I was hanging up a picture for the wife, and the chair went over. I fell and broke my arm and cut my face' was the reply. Ginger burst out laughing at this. 'It's nothing to laugh at y'know, I was carted off to hospital. Anyway, what are you doing here? doesn't seem to be much wrong with you.' Ginger replied 'I came off a motor cycle at near 120 mph and sprained my thumb.'

We all laughed heartily at this, and I think the other rider was also reassured.

On race day the weather was not too good, with mist on the Mountain, so the stewards decided to postpone the start for a couple of hours. We duly started and conditions were much improved for a while. But the mist came down again later and made visibility worse than before. Another Bemsee member, J. McDonnell, (Mac to us) was also staying at Cunningham's and had agreed to look after my pit. When I came into refuel at the end of the 3rd lap Mac was jubilant. 'Keep going just as you are' was his advice. 'You're lying sixth and about 10 minutes inside replica time'. The pit stop cost me 61 seconds and I had two more laps to do. As the mist came down, everyone's lap times got longer, except mine. I was getting more familiar with the course each lap and the cycle was going smoothly.

I completed lap five in 34 minutes, 21 seconds, at approximately 66 mph, my fastest yet. Bill Beamish, who had been in Jack Shenston's pit, had now transferred to mine, to cheer me home on my last lap. The unfortunate Jack had been the first out of the race on lap 1, somewhere around Creg Willeys Hill, where he had gone through the hedge!

But it was not to be. Approaching East Snaefell Gate up on the mountain in the midst, I could not see the left hander in time, and banking over too much and too late, I came off. A doctor and nurse were at the spot, and would not hear of me continuing. Another retired rider had dashed out and grabbed the cycle as it lay, revving its heart out. He told me he had shut it off and brought it in, and that it was OK.

I was out of the race, with nine more miles to go, and had sufficient time in hand to have been able to walk round that corner and still get in, in time. Such is the hazard of the TT course to a newcomer, when the mist comes down. I finished up in Ramsey hospital to have stitches inserted in my forehead, arm and chin. They were all for keeping me there for a few days, but Bill Beamish hired a car, and came out to visit me, having other ideas. He planned to take me back with him, explaining to the ward sister that we were due to leave the Island on the next morning's boat and promised her he'd look after the patient. Reluctantly she agreed, and I wasn't sorry to be leaving with him. I looked a bit more of a mess than usual, but most people's verdict was 'Oh! he'll live.' We collected our two cycles, both very much the worse for their prangs, neither being rideable. The IOM Steam Packet Co landed us safely at Liverpool. Nearing the quay I said 'Over there Bill, there's the menace'. He nodded and observed 'I told you that no one would want the bloody thing. Only an oil baron could afford the oil for it'.

The race was won by Denis Parkinson on a 248 cc Excelsior at 69.8 mph. He had also won the previous year and a win the year following completed the hat trick. The other places in the 1937 event were:

Passing under the Hawker Bridge spanning the Byfleet banking. The Author, 248 cc Excelsior (21), keeps well inside the 10 foot line whilst Dennis Loveday, 497 cc Ariel (2), and E. Fullam, 499 cc Vincent HRD (10), thunder by *(Motor Cycle)*

2nd H.M. Rowell - 249 cc Rudge - 68.45 mph
3rd L. Longstaff - 246 cc CTS - 67.28 mph
4th S.M. Miller - 249 cc OK Supreme - 66.65 mph
5th J.A. Worswick - 248 cc Excelsior - 64.96 mph
Fastest lap D. Parkinson 71.31 mph

Checking through the lap times, most people's best was their second or third as the mist came down from then on. However, my best was my fifth, in 34 minutes 21 seconds, when I was getting more familiar with the course. This was approximately 66 mph, and my lap times, excluding the lap with the pit stop, were getting faster by ten seconds a lap.

Throughout the race I was sixth, about four minutes ahead of the seventh man, R.M. Board, on another Excelsior. I certainly did not slow up on my last lap, so I should have been sixth at approx. 64.4 mph and Board would then have been seventh at 63.58 mph. R.S. Simpson on a 248 cc Excelsior was seventh and he was the last one to gain a Replica. At the end of lap five, I was about 5 minutes ahead of him, so I was in a very comfortable position for my Replica when I threw the model away.

I was the last one in the race to retire, and had finished the climb up the Mountain, so it was mostly downhill to the finish. Although, of course, it was a bitter disappointment to have my Replica snatched from me at the eleventh hour like that, I did not really fare so badly. The first three, particularly H.M. Rowell, who lived on the Island, were much more familiar with the course. To be in sixth position in such company as this was certainly no disgrace. The tricky and difficult Isle of Man course requires more than one Manx Grand Prix and its practicing, to enable one to lap it at the best speed.

Of the twelve Excelsiors in the race that day, I would have been third. The rest of the field comprised seven New Imperials, five OK Supremes, four Rudges, two CTS's and a solitary Sunbeam.

The 10 lap Mountain race at Brooklands on 8th October 1938. The Author, 248 cc Excelsior (16), about to pass J. McDonnell, 248 cc Bickell JAP, on the Member's Hill turn, to take the race and the class 6 and A Aggregate Cup *(Motor Cycle)*

The 10 lap Mountain race on 8th October 1938. The same corner from a different angle. J. McDonnell (17) and the Author (16) *(Motor Cycle)*

83

This was my one and only visit to the Isle of Man as a competitor. I enjoyed it immensely. It made a nice change from the short circuit racing with which I was familiar. It also made me realise what a difficult course it is to learn. On lap four, between Sulby and Ramsey, I came across a left hander unawares. There was nothing for it but to lay the model right over as I was going too fast for the line I was taking. I laid the model over until the footrest scraped the ground, an unbelievable angle on that cycle. The Excelsior responded nobly, and went round as if it were on rails. Only the superb handling of that TT replica cycle prevented disaster on that corner. When it did lay down on the Mountain during the next lap, loose gravel was present in the gutter, and the road was wet from the mist.

We arrived home without further incident, and the casualties were parked in the woods. Peter arrived to inspect his new purchase. 'What's up with the engine Bert' he asked me. 'Nothing' I said, 'Why do you ask?'. 'It's solid' he said. And so it was, unknown to any of us. I straight away got busy and lifted the cylinder head. The exhaust valve head had parted from the stem, with the usual effect on the rest of the power plant. The cylinder head was replaced and the engine removed complete and returned to the Excelsior works. Peter had not even heard his engine running!

Soon afterwards we heard that Peter's firm was no more, having passed into the Receiver's hands. The Excelsior had been supplied on HP so we had to repossess it. After some time we offered the finance company a nominal sum for it, and they agreed. Bill suggested that as I had been its only rider, I should acquire it and race it next year. After consideration I thought this might be a good idea, so I paid up and the Excelsior was mine. The only things to acquire were sundry sprockets, plugs and a Brooklands pipe and silencer, all being supplied by the works.

At this stage I should state that the bronze head had triple coil valve springs to each valve, and a bottom seating plug. This latter dispensed with the usual plug washer, making a joint at its lowest extremity, level with the electrode. The head itself had quite a small hole into the combustion chamber, which had been counterbored to receive the thread for the plug, leaving a small horizontal shelf of metal on which the plug bottomed. I hope I've made this clear!

The log book records reads:- Engine No. BRAR 117, Model FR 11, bore 67 mm, stroke 70.5 mm, 248 cc. Compression ratio 9.1 to 1 for 50/50 mixture. Weight 295 lbs. 22.5 bhp at peak revs of 7350 rpm. Gear ratios for IOM 6.22, 6.77, 8.7 and 12.09 to 1.

The Hutchinson Hundred held on 8th October 1938. No. 19 is G.H. Hayden 348 cc Velocette and No. 4, E.R. Evans 498 cc BSA *(Motor Cycle)*

'Local racing school' rider Norman Cox, photographed during 1938 with his sluggish 348 cc Norton referred to in the text. He lost his life over the English Channel during 1940 in a Lysander aircraft *(Motor Cycle)*

My first outing was at the Brooklands Road Circuit on 12th March 1938. Ebby evidently thought the Excelsior was at least equal to the Ariel. I was given 1 minute 1 second start on scratch in both races, and my best lap of 58.71 mph was not good enough to put me in the first six in either race. Comment in the log book, 'Too much of a jump between second and third ratios.'

Its next outing was on March 26th at Gatwick, dealt with in the Chapter on that course. Suffice to say that it won the Experts class and was 2nd in both Experts Barred, and the Handicap. Brooklands was again visited on April 2nd, round the Mountain this time. For this I had increased the size of the rear drive sprocket by two teeth, bringing top gear down to 6.44. Ebby again frowned on me and I was unplaced in both 5 and 10 lap races, my best lap being at 62.86 mph.

The Campbell Circuit was visited once more on 14th May, when the Brooklands Road Championships were held. There was no Lightweight Championship but I managed a sixth place in the first Long Handicap, and a fifth place in the second Long Handicap, being unplaced in either of the Short Handicap Races. My best lap was 59.31 mph, slightly faster than the first time. I also had a bent exhaust valve for the whole of the meeting; this had also occurred in the first race at the previous Mountain Meeting. As my best laps were in the last race each time, the bent valve apparently made no difference. The valve would touch the piston if the revs exceeded the 8,000 mark; each time I took off the head and fitted a new valve. Even if it didn't make any difference, I couldn't reassemble an engine with a bent exhaust valve! I had quite a nice stock of the bent variety by the end of the season. The makers gave the life of an exhaust valve as 400 miles.

Upon reading *The Motor Cycle* report of this meeting, I noticed that I was having a ding dong scrap for two laps with R.E. Geeson, on another 248 cc Excelsior. The report then continues:- 'Meanwhile, L.E. Brooks (348 cc Velocette), 25 seconds, had been putting in some useful work and managed to catch Geeson on the last lap. Perryman failed to appear and third place went to H.P. Deschamps, 348 cc Norton. The winner's speed was 56.01 mph.'

A fine view of the Campbell circuit at Bridge Corner, with the Sahara Straight in the background. Beyond that can be seen the end of the Members Banking and on the skyline, the main railway line of the Southern Railway which gave its name to the Railway Straight of the old Outer Circuit. M.D. Whitworth (7) is riding a 497 cc Triumph twin *(Motor Cycle)*

L.J. Archer, Velocette (4), is about to pass Guy Newman, Velocette (20), as they leave the Test Hill hairpin. Archer finished second and Newman fifth in this, the Event 6 Handicap Race of the 12th March 1938 meeting *(Motor Cycle)*

Actually, according to the official Brooklands results, I finished fifth, collecting eight points towards the 250 cc Aggregate Cup, which I won at the end of the season. Two fifth places in races such as these would give you as many points as the winner of one race.

For 23rd July there were 3 races only at Brooklands, the Lightweight, Junior and Senior Grands Prix, and these were on the International calendar. I entered the Lightweight, and H.G. Tyrell-Smith was also in it with a 'works' Excelsior taving hairpin valve springs. This proved much faster than mine, and got away from me at the start. As I rounded Aerodrome Curve, I could see a large cloud of dust arising and just visible at the top of it was Tyrell's grinning face surmounted by his shamrock-adorned crash helmet. Good, I thought, that's one I shan't have to worry about, he's run off the course onto the grass.

Some three laps later, I had just shut off for the Test Hill hairpin and was braking, when I was amazed to see Tyrell come past with the power still on! He negotiated the hairpin safely, so his brakes must also have been superior to mine.

I had no hope of catching Les Archer's New Imperial which held the 250 class course record, and won at 61.81 mph. Tyrell was second, and Dave Whitworth third. I was pleased to be in 4th place in so important a race.

One of our local riders, Norman Cox, had a 348 cc Manx Norton, on which he was a rather poor performer on the Outer Circuit. He asked me to give it a try round the Mountain, which I did; but I could do no better with it than he did. It was decidedly sluggish, and in all my racing career, that was the one and only time that I was Norton mounted. I also tried Bill Beamish's 246 cc New Imperial round the Mountain. It was a lot slower than Les Archer's version. I could lap faster on my own Excelsior.

After the Gatwick meeting in June, and the Brighton Speed Trials in July, my last meeting was on October 8th, at Brooklands, for a five lap race and ten lap Mountain Handicap Race. I was unplaced in the first, but in the ten lapper, the last Mountain race of the season, and the last one in which I was to ride the Excelsior, I had a fine scrap with my old pal J. McDonnell (Mac) on his Bickell JAP. We were both limit men, and had a two minutes two seconds start on the scratch man, Ron Harris, who was riding a bored out 502 cc Norton. I realised that at last I had a favourable handicap, and with a bit of luck could annexe this race. I was No 16 and Mac No 17, and after I had shaken him off, I was not further challenged, to romp home the winner. This was the only Brooklands race I ever won with the Excelsior, a fitting finale to my 250 season.

My future wife, Connie, came along to this meeting with me, her first Brooklands visit, so the victory was even more welcome! It also clinched the Aggregate Cup for me in classes 6 and A, the 16 points I collected for this win enabling me to overhaul Les Archer by 3 points! Second man was R.E. Geeson, on another Excelsior, off the 1 minute 53 seconds mark, whilst Mac managed to romp home in third place. My winning speed was 61.05 mph.

So my Excelsior finished in a blaze of glory, and I sold it to Norman Cox, the owner of the sluggish Norton. I had enjoyed a very trouble-free season with it as it was very reliable, if not as fast as the best 250's. In fairness to it, I was always on petrol benzol, which put it at a disadvantage round the Mountain when matched against the alcohol motors.

My 14 1/2 stone in riding gear made me hardly the best jockey for a little 'un. Our other local rider, Basil Keys, weighed about 10 stone. He could have taken a light pillion passenger and still carried but little more weight than me. I also missed the lively performance of my late five hundred.

Before closing the Excelsior saga, one other incident is worth recording. My local club, the Brighton and District, had organised a hill climb and invited me along. Connie came with me, and we towed the trailer with the 'Ex' on board behind my Morris 12.

Arriving at the site, I was adamant. I would not even bother to unload the 'Ex' from its trailer. The course went straight up the side of the South Downs, and must have been about 1 in 2 at its steepest part. The start was a short way up the opposite slope, to enable competitors to get a run at the hill. I doubted very much if the 'Ex' would get halfway up. It had ordinary road racing tyres, as I had never raced it on the grass. But the lads dearly wanted to see it in action and they finally prevailed on me to have a go.

I knew I wouldn't have to change out of bottom, and I could go to 8,000 on the rev counter with safety. Down the slope I charged and as soon as the revs. reached the 8,000 mark I eased and held them, and the little 'Ex' shot up that hill as if it were level, the revs falling to only 6,500 at the top. It made the

Entering the Test Hill hairpin in the Event 4 Handicap Race of 12th March 1938. L.J. Archer, 348 cc Velocette (3), finished in sixth place *(Motor Cycle)*

In the Senior Mountain Championship of 3rd September 1938, J.O. Finch, 495 cc AJS, keeps well clear as W.R. Lunn, 348 cc Velocette (4), gets uncomfortably close to an unidentified Norton at the Members Hill turn. The Norton's front wheel is clear of the ground! *(Motor Cycle)*

Sir Malcolm Campbell rides his 496 cc Triumph Speed Twin on the track during an interval at the meeting held on the 3rd September 1938 *(Motor Cycle)*

fastest time of the day easily, much to my amazement. Everyone else had to change into second and then back again when well up. Some missed the gear, and stalled!

Although no megaphone was fitted it behaved as if there was one. When getting away the motor was quite sluggish until the rev. counter reached 4,500, when it felt as if someone kicked you in the back, giving fantastic acceleration.

Another thing to undergo change was the race transport. Upon my joining the staff of Beamish Bros., our faithful lorry was discontinued and I used the firm's trailer, towed by whatever car was available. I was running a Morris 8 at the time when I acquired the Excelsior, and I decided to construct my own lightweight trailer to take my mount, independent of the firm's, as the latter was often required when I was away racing.

I obtained an Austin 7 front axle, and after locking the stub axle movement, fixed a channel shape length of car chassis longitudinally to the centre of it. Two substantial brackets were also added, to accept the footrests, which were bolted down to same. A drawbar attachment, spring loaded, was attached to the front end, and this in turn was coupled to the Morris's rear bumper, suitably strengthened back to the chassis.

The first trip with this outfit revealed that trailer and cycle weighed almost as much as the car, and being unbraked, tended to push the car along during braking. I therefore exchanged the 8 for a Morris 12, and with this heavier and more powerful car, no further trouble was experienced.

Having disposed of the Excelsior to Norman Cox, and having no mount of my own to ride for the first meeting of 1939, I lent him the trailer, to transport the Excelsior to Brooklands. Norman's car was an Alvis Speed Twenty and his wife, Connie, had been a member of the Brooklands Riley ladies' team. She was driving on this fateful day, and we went via Brighton to pick up my Connie from her office, who took up position on the rear seat with me. The Alvis was a much more formidable prime mover than my Morris, and time was getting short. On the road to Dorking, Connie decided to make up for lost time, and I noticed the trailer was doing its best to imitate a kangaroo on several occasions.

Unaccustomed to this treatment, the trailer decided to signify its disapproval by divorcing itself from its drawbar. Looking out from my side window I perceived the trailer about to overtake us on the nearside. 'The trailer's loose' I burst out. 'Pull out in the centre of the road and put your foot down Connie' I advised. Luckily she did just that, without question. The balance being roughly equal over the axle, first the front and then the rear of that central member touched the road. At last, the jagged front end caught in a hole in the road surface and the whole outfit described a semi-circular orbit, landing on the Excelsior's handlebars and racing saddle, the trailer wheels still rapidly revolving.

Connie remained in the Alvis, and we disembarked and ran back to the calamity. The handlebars were bent and the rear mudguard was stove in, so that the bike was not operational. The trailer alignment had been seriously affected also, so the complete outfit was left in the charge of a roadside garage, which conveniently happened to be adjacent. We continued up to the track to become spectators, and the following day I went back with the firm's car and trailer. With Norman's help, I unshackled the Excelsior and secured it safely in the other trailer. The remains of my own trailer were dismantled and also stowed aboard, all being returned to our works for attention.

The Excelsior was soon dealt with, the damage being only superficial. The trailer I eventually rebuilt, with added stiffening in the vital places, and used it to convey the Ariel when I raced it.

During the 1938 season, I was approached at Brooklands by R.E. Geeson, who also raced an Excelsior. He was forming the Bar One MCC and asked me if I would care to join. Membership was open to anyone, providing they didn't ride a Norton! As I had enjoyed quite a few successes without the aid of this famous marque, he thought I would set a good example!

There is no doubt that Nortons were the most usual winners of the races at that time, but even so, other makes gave them a very good run for it, particularly Velocettes. As I have always preferred anything out of the usual run of things, I managed without a Norton. But still I did not become a member of the Bar One MCC!

Chapter Seven

The Gatwick Speed Trials

In 1931 The Sunbeam MCC inaugurated their Gatwick Speed Trials. These took place on a private tarmac road, leading from the main London to Brighton road, the A23, to the stables for the Gatwick horse racing course. All this, of course, is no more, being within the boundaries of Gatwick Airport.

To return to the Speed Trials. A course was marked out for 440 yards, and a third line was situated 10 yards from the start. A thin tape was stretched across the course at the start of the 440 mark and when a competitor broke this, it set the timing apparatus in motion. A similar tape at the other end, on being broken, stopped the timing. This timing system was designed by the Sunbeam Club, and was accurate to two places of decimals, being electrically operated. In effect, the event was a standing start 450 yards, timed over the last 440.

These trials were an immediate success. Regular Brooklands riders appeared alongside the rawest of tyro's, so classes were made for Experts, Experts Barred and Newcomers. There was also a special invitation event for the six fastest riders, to wind up the meeting. The awards for the latter were:- First, a quart tankard - second, a 1 pint tankard - third, a half pint tankard - fourth, fifth and sixth, ashtrays. Thus you were sure of an award if you qualified for this event.

If Eric Fernihough, with his unblown Brough Superior, or Noel Pope with his supercharged Brough Superior were present, then they invariably won this event. Unless, that is, as once happened, the start was so slippery as to make this potent machinery uncontrollable, allowing a 500 to win.

In all other events it was first, a 1 pint tankard - second a half pint tankard - third, an ashtray. No money at all could be won.

Everyone thoroughly enjoyed themselves at these very matey meetings, which were nearly always blessed with traditional Sunbeam weather. I went originally as a spectator, and was present, in August 1933, when Eric Fernihough on his immaculate 498 cc Excelsior JAP established a 500 cc course record of 12.54 seconds. As far as I remember, this record was never broken. Eric was an expert at sprint work, and if he was present at any meeting, he invariable won his class. On this particular run, he was so skilful with his starting technique, that he lifted his front wheel over the tape and broke it with the rear of his machine, saving valuable 'hundredths.'

The assessment of the Expert was rather erratic. For the 500 cc class you had to cover the course in 13 seconds or less. That was within 0.46 seconds of the course record! For 350's you were deemed Expert if you clocked 15.00 seconds or less, the 350 course record being 13.26 seconds. Therefore in this class there was a margin of 1.74 seconds. For 250's the Expert rating was 17.00 seconds and the course record here was 15.25 seconds, 1.75 seconds below Expert status.

I first competed with my 497 cc Ariel in August 1935, and every time the Ariel was at Gatwick it reached the six fastest event, once finishing as the fastest 500 cc at 13.18 seconds, beaten only by Noel Pope's supercharged Brough. Yet it never put me in the Experts category. I therefore suggested to F.W. Pinhard, the Club's secretary, that the 500 cc Expert time should be amended to 13.50 seconds, still about one whole second slower than the record. The Sunbeam Club's committee evidently agreed with me, for the 1938 figure was so altered, and the first time I took my new Ariel to Gatwick, I became an Expert with a run at 13.43 seconds.

The figures, of course, would vary from meeting to meeting, because of wind strength on the course, for or against you. Even so, you had to be consistent to win, and over five years my award winning ten runs showed a variation of from 13.18 to 13.62 seconds, only 0.44 seconds between them. Realising this, in 1938, Francis Beart, the famous Brooklands tuner and a regular competitor at Gatwick, presented an award for consistency. This was won by F. Harper on a 500 cc Triumph with 0.06 seconds between four runs, two exactly the same! My 250 cc Excelsior was runner up, with 0.12 seconds variation.

At the 20th May meeting in 1939, I won this same award, this time on my new 497 cc Ariel, with a variation of 0.11 seconds between four runs.

Of the early meetings at Gatwick, the times recorded were improved on in later years, with one exception. Eric Fernihough's brilliant run on the fine 498 cc Excelsior JAP, when he recorded 12.54 seconds, was never broken. The last meeting in which Eric rode this 500 at Gatwick was 24th March 1934 as far as I can trace, when he returned 12.73 seconds; but after rain in the morning the drying tarmac had made the start greasy. Eric used an old racing tyre this day, and he energetically cut this about to increase its grip, and also ran it at very low pressure. Even so, at the start the rear tyre steamed for a good thirty yards, proving that he was still suffering considerable wheelspin. Eric also won the 350 cc class at this meeting on his 344 cc Excelsior JAP, in 14.23 seconds, from H.J. Bacon's Velocette, which took 14.93 seconds, and D.J. Maloney's Velocette which recorded 14.94 seconds. Classes were often won, (or lost!) at these meetings by 1/100 th of a second. In these early days, people like Francis Beart and Frank Williams, formidable exponents in later years, were still classed as Non-Experts. So was Basil Keys, the ultimate holder of the 350 course record. At this meeting his 349 cc Rudge took 15.23 seconds to give him third place in the 350 Experts Barred class.

An indifferent start would exclude you from a place even on a machine capable of winning that class. The condition of the course would account for differences between one meeting and the next, and, of course, some riders had found just that little extra to turn the tables on their rivals. No one seemed to mind, and everyone agreed that it was great fun. There was no animosity. Everyone was on the most friendly terms with his deadliest rival!

In 1935 I decided to join in the fun, instead of spectating, and went along on 13th April with my then new 497 cc Ariel. Fresh from its triumphs of the previous week at Brooklands Clubman's Day, it was still on petrol fuel, against the local alcohol fiends.

The start of the timed 440 yards Gatwick Speed Trials on 20th May 1939. J. Henry, 498 cc supercharged Triumph twin, about to break the starting tape *(J.H. Pigneguy)*

Basil Keys gets his 348 cc Velocette away at the Gatwick Speed Trials *(Motor Cycling)*

The Motor Cycle reported:- 'In the 500 cc class there were many as-you-can-buy machines, notably Ariels, in the hands of W.J. Blake, S. Stubbings and A.C. Perryman; Stubbings was extraordinarily rapid.' Be that as it may, my single-port 1935 model always had the edge on Stuart's 1934 two-port model, but as no times are recorded for any of the Ariels, I must leave it at that. Suffice it to say that after this meeting, when I had changed over to alcohol fuel, there was no other single cylinder Ariel that could equal, let only surpass, the times that I recorded.

More and more famous names from Brooklands continued to arrive to sample the Sunbeam Club's particular brand of speed revelry. This meeting saw the first appearance of Ben Bickell with the supercharged 500 cc Ariel four, the only **Ariel** ever to push mine into second place. At this meeting Ben was classed as a Non-Expert (sic!) and he screamed down the course to win the Experts Barred cup in 12.59 seconds, only 0.05 sec. slower than the 500 cc record! Other Bemsee newcomers were M.D. Whitworth, who bagged the 350 cc Non-Experts (again sic!) with his famous 348 cc Rex Acme Blackburne in 14.43 seconds. C.K. Mortimer, brought his 498 cc Grindlay-Peerless JAP into second place, in 13.50 seconds, behind another Bemsee star A.J. Rawlence, 490 cc Norton (13.34 seconds), who won the 500 cc Experts Barred class. These famous names tended to make the latter class name something of a laughing stock and even after this, the latter two were still eligible as they had not bettered 13.00 seconds. Ben, of course, became an Expert. His time was the second best ever recorded by a 500 cc bike.

Basil Keys, this time on a 348 cc Velocette, showed his mettle by pushing Eric's Excelsior into second place in the 350 Open class. Their times were 13.86 and 13.94 seconds respectively. Another Bemsee exponent, I.B. Wickstead, brought his 250 cc Mechanical Marvel Excelsior into second place in the open Newcomer's Event, with a time of 16.01 seconds, behind the 348 cc AJS of A.J. Fabbrini, who clocked 15.16 seconds. N.R. Illingworth cut his time to 15.60 seconds, in winning the 250 cc Open class, whilst Frank Wiliams's Cotton carried off the 500 cc open in 13.00 seconds, just beating Murray Smith's 13.11 seconds on a Rudge.

This meeting told us why we had not seen Eric's 500 cc Excelsior for twelve months. He had been busy with a much more potent piece of machinery, in the form of a 996 cc unsupercharged Brough Superior, with which he now proceeded to smash the Unlimited Sidecar Class record with 14.33

John Henry with his supercharged Triumph at Gatwick in May 1939 *(J.H. Pigneguy)*

Gatwick 20th May 1939. John Henry lifts the front wheel of his 500 cc supercharged Triumph as he breaks the tape to start the timing gear *(J.H. Pigneguy)*

seconds. Having done that, Eric removed the chair and took the Brough down solo to win the Unlimited Class in 11.72 seconds. Ben's Ariel Four was second in 12.59 seconds. Eric also established a new course record of 11.72 seconds, the first rider to complete the course in under 12.00 seconds!

For the next meeting of 17th August 1935, I started with the Ariel on my long sequence of award winning, and Gatwick became one of my happy hunting grounds. Eric Fernihough had presented a Challenge Cup for the fastest Non-Expert at the meeting, and I collected this with a run in 13.52 seconds.

Chief topic of conversation at this meeting was the state of the surface, which had been given a top dressing of tar and granite chips too recently for the chips to have bedded in. Right up to starting time industrious officials brushed the course near the start. This, of course, affected speeds, which were all down on last time, Ferni winning the Unlimited Sidecars in 14.62 seconds, and the Solos in 12.55 seconds against his 14.33 and 11.72 seconds of the previous meeting. Eric again won the 350 cc Experts, but in the slower time of 14.23 seconds. The Non-Experts in this capacity fell to my old enemy of the Junior Grand Prix, Dennis Loveday, who took his Velocette down in 14.95 seconds, to become an Expert in the process.

For the 500 cc Experts event, Ben Bickell's supercharged four annexed the honours in 13.19 seconds, whilst my unblown 497 cc Ariel was second with 13.62 seconds. A.J. Rawlence, 490 cc Norton, won the Non-Experts in 13.66 seconds, from L.E. Good, 499 cc Rudge. The Unlimited Solo went to Eric, with 12.55 seconds, and Noel Pope's blown Brough 12.77 seconds, whilst my Ariel took the Unlimited Solos (Experts Barred) in 13.52 seconds with A.J. Rawlence second on his Norton. Eric won the Gatwick Challenge Cup for fastest time of the day, and as already reported, I gained the Fernihough Challenge Cup for the fastest Non-Expert. Altogether a very successful day for my first sprint meeting using alcohol fuel.

28th March 1936 was notable for a new course record by Ferni in 11.57 seconds. About two thirds of the way down his rear tyre punctured; the wheel tore out the valve and security bolt and started to spin inside the tyre. Eric thought that the wheel bumping on the road was a big end knock (!) but he kept the throttle wide open and only realised that the tyre had punctured when he came to slow down.

Local rider J. Henry took my old 348 cc Velocette (ex-H.C. Lamacraft) down in 15.29 seconds to win the 350 cc Newcomer's Event. F.W.S. Clarke took the Newcomers 500 cc class, with a 497 cc Ariel, in 13.67 seconds.

Basil Keys again won the 350 class on his Velocette in 14.21 seconds from C.K. Mortimer's 348 cc Norton. I managed to bring my own Mark IV Velocette into second place in the Experts barred class with a time of 15.29 seconds. The Broughs of Eric and Noel Pope were first and second in the Unlimited Class, the former, of course, again winning the Gatwick Cup, whilst the Fernihough cup went to I.B. Wickstead, the fastest Non-Expert with 12.68 seconds.

By now these meetings had settled down to a steady pattern and the same names of the regulars appeared time and again, the only difference being that the pack sometimes got reshuffled.

Great excitement occurred at the 8th August 1936 meeting, when Francis Beart and Noel Pope, both on 490 cc Nortons, tied for first place in the 500 cc open class with a time of 13.19 seconds. As everybody had two runs in each class, the aggregate of both runs was taken, making Noel the victor.

The Unlimited Class naturally went to Eric's Brough, this time in 11.80 seconds, whilst C.K. Mortimer did well to finish second to the maestro in 13.10 seconds. Francis Beart, this time on a 490 cc Norton, took the Unlimited Experts Barred in 13.21 seconds and I managed to bring my 497 cc Ariel into second place, with 13.59 seconds.

According to *The Motor Cycle* report, 'A.C. Perryman (497 cc Ariel) gave the crowd a thrill when starting, for his machine literally leapt on its tail and he lost valuable *seconds* (my italics) before he got going properly.' If this were true, if only I could have made a perfect start, who knows? I might even have taken the course record away from Eric!!

The 1937 season had started well for me with my 1st and 2nd place Round the Mountain at Brooklands on 17th April.

The following Saturday, 24th April, saw the Ariel once more at Gatwick, and it was to make its fastest run ever on this day. The weather was dull with a slight headwind, and the compression ratio had been increased from that of the previous week to 12.96 to 1. There was some slight misfiring later in the day, probably due to an oily plug. However, times of 13.18, 13.29, 13.30, 13.33 and 13.50 seconds (on the misfiring run) were recorded.

In the Open events, local rider T.L. Beamish took his 246 cc New Imperial down in 15.81 seconds to win, whilst another of our locals, J. Henry, turned the tables on fellow club member Basil Keys, by clocking 14.98 seconds on his 348 cc AJS so becoming an Expert, against the latter's Velocette time of 15.18 seconds.

The Six Fastest today were Noel's Brough, in 12.11 seconds, Frank Williams 13.16 seconds, Francis Beart 13.20 seconds, C.K. Mortimer 13.29 seconds, fifth Johnny Waite and sixth myself, on my Ariel.

For the meeting of 7th August 1937 I decided to make a determined attempt to join the select band of Experts in the 500 cc class, i.e. those who had covered the course in 13.00 seconds or less. At the previous meeting on 24th April, I had managed 13.18 seconds and conditions had not been ideal. I decided to raise the compression ratio still further, so I removed all the compression plates, pushing it up to 13.75 to 1.

The day was very hot, and there was a slight headwind. I also used a 21 tooth engine sprocket instead of my usual 22 tooth. This proved too low, and made the getaway difficult, through wheelspin. The lower gear enabled the engine to over-rev, with the inevitable result; the exhaust valve embraced the piston. So, the times recorded were inferior instead of improved.

Francis Beart had a supercharged 499 cc Douglas, and the noise of this was terrific, rivalling that of Noel Pope's supercharged Brough. Even this potent blown twin did not make Francis an Expert. He won the 600 cc Experts Barred event, with a time of 13.62 seconds, the same as my time two years previously.

For the Experts class, Noel Pope wheeled out his 498 cc Pope JAP and took first place in 12.88 seconds. Francis improved on his time and finished second, this time in 13.37 seconds. Tom Pullin's 498 cc Excelsior JAP annexed third place, in 13.49 seconds.

The Ariel certainly was not at its best, so during the tea interval I decided on drastic measures. The head was removed, revealing an exhaust valve seating on one side only. With nothing to lose, I gave the offender a hearty crack with my 2 lb hammer! This certainly improved matters, but I would not like to say that the valve now seated 100%. The head was hastily replaced, the 21 tooth sprocket removed and the 22 tooth re-instated.

The 600 cc times were no better, but in the Unlimited Class Noel's Brough returned 12.19 seconds to take first place, and I managed to gain second place with 13.42 seconds. Francis brought the blown Douglas into third place in 13.52 seconds.

I feel that *The Motor Cycle* report for this meeting is worth quoting:- 'A.C. Perryman was not satisfied with the running of his Ariel in the first session, so during the tea interval he removed the cylinder head and dealt a severe blow to a guilty valve stem. The treatment was effective, for Perryman gained second place in the Unlimited class. The winner was Pope on the supercharged Brough (12.19 seconds) but Perryman also distinguished himself by some very quick motoring. The meeting finished with a race for the six fastest riders however, and Pope won this with the highly creditable time of 12.01 seconds. The runner up in this event was Perryman, who also had the honour of being the fastest Non-Expert.'

This was to be the last run of my beloved Ariel at this very friendly meeting, and even now I was still not an Expert! As a matter of interest, the course record was held by Eric Fernihough with the unsupercharged Brough at 11.57 seconds, only 0.97 seconds faster than his 500 cc course record.

The Manx Grand Prix occupied me for the next few weeks, and when I returned, regretfully I decided to part with my faithful Ariel. I sold it to Reg Whatman of Hastings, who, believe it or not, planned to use it in trials, the type of event in which it first started life in my hands. So the wheel had turned a full circle. I have no record of how Reg fared with it, but it had served me well!

The 1938 season commenced on 12th March at Brooklands and the first Gatwick meeting followed on the 26th. I could see that I would have to learn a completely new starting technique on the little Excelsior if I were to figure in the awards list. Unlike the Ariel, which had tremendous power, and quite a low bottom gear, the power had to be treated with respect, or the machine would most likely finish up on the fence.

Bottom gear was only a shade lower than the Ariel's road gear, and with the latter in Gatwick trim it

Johnny Lockett on F. Beart's 490 cc Norton at Gatwick in May 1939 *(B.E. Keys)*

Francis Beart and his 490 cc Norton at Gatwick in 1939 *(B.E. Keys)*

had an even lower gear than the 250. So it had to be helped off the line with some energetic foot work reminiscent of the early belt drive riders paddle-starting their mounts. Also, this little fellow was swamped by my ungainly bulk and weight, and was still further handicapped with its petrol benzol fuel against the alcohol type of the faster contestants. With a compression ratio of only 9 to 1, I did not expect any very high placings. To be equal to the Ariel's 12.96, I should need about 15 to 1!

However, it must have made up further down the course what it lost at the start, as I won the 250 cc Open class in 17.06 seconds, and finished second in the Experts Barred event in 16.95 seconds. The winner of this latter proved to be H.R. Nash's world record breaking 146 cc New Imperial, in 16.79 seconds, ridden this day by R.G. Hunt.

I also annexed second place in the Handicap, which R.G. Hunt won with a time of 14.74 seconds on handicap. On top of this, as already related, I was runner-up for the Consistency Award, with only a 0.12 variation between my 4 runs. It made me an Expert at my first attempt, the best run being 16.95 seconds, in spite of a headwind that day.

There had been other changes during the winter in our local racing school, apart from myself blossoming forth on a 250. John Henry had fitted a small Arnott supercharger to his 346 cc AJS, running at 7/10ths engine speed, the second member of this marque that John had blown. It was, of course, experimental, but we hoped it would do things later on. At the last Gatwick meeting John had the edge on Basil Key's Velocette and had become an Expert with the Ajay in unblown form.

Basil was not likely to relish this state of affairs, so he had hied him along to Ron Harris's emporium in Maidenhead, and exchanged the Velo for a 348 cc Norton, now discarded from Noel Pope's stable. Armed with this new machinery, Basil proceeded to break the 350 cc course record with a run in 13.76 seconds.

This upset another Bemsee rider in the person of S.H. Goddard, and he signified his disapproval by taking his 346 OK Supreme JAP down in 13.64 seconds. This was not the end of the saga however. As Basil got more accustomed to his new machinery, he displaced Goddard into second place by clocking 13.61 seconds to win the 350 Open Class.

Later in the afternoon, the wind, which had troubled us earlier on, subsided into a gentle breeze, and Basil's rapid motoring had earned him a place in the Six Fastest. This, of course, was won by Noel Pope on the Brough, in 11.87 seconds. Tom Pullin had removed the chair from his 590 cc JAP outfit, to clock 12.94 seconds in solo form, whilst Frank's fire engine took third place with 13.19 seconds.

Basil took the 350 cc Norton along against the lighter breeze, to gain fourth place behind Frank, and shatter the 350 record once again with his run of 13.50 seconds. This was probably the best day ever for our local racing school at Gatwick.

Out total bag was:

250 cc Experts   1st A.C. Perryman, 248 cc Excelsior 17.06 seconds
250 cc Experts Barred   2nd A.C. Perryman, 248 cc Excelsior 16.95 seconds
250 cc Handicap   2nd A.C. Perryman, 248 cc Excelsior 17.25 seconds
Beart Cup (consistency award). Runner up A.C. Perryman, Excelsior, variation 0.12 seconds
350 cc Experts   1st B.E. Keys, 348 cc Norton 13.61 seconds
350 cc Handicap   1st B.E. Keys, 348 cc Norton 14.14 seconds
Sidecar Handicap   1st J. Hempson, 990 AJS 16.69 seconds
Six Fastest Riders:- 4th B.E. Keys, 348 cc Norton 13.50 seconds and course record.

The second meeting for 1938 was billed for 28th May instead of the usual August date. The clerk of the weather, however, had other ideas and it rained in torrents; this caused the meeting to be postponed for three weeks, until 18th June, which made it clash with TT week in the Isle of Man. All *The Motor Cycle* reporters must have been on the Island, as there is very scant information as to what happened at Gatwick that Saturday.

Francis Beart at last became an Expert as a result of my pointing out to the organisers how ridiculous was the timing of the Experts category. 0.50 seconds had been added to the 600 cc class, so Francis's four runs of 13.60, 13.40, 13.48 and 13.49 seconds won him his own cup for the Consistency Award, and made him an Expert as well!

A remarkable performance was that of veteran Frank Williams, in winning the Six Fastest event in 12.55 seconds. He came within 1/10th of a second of Ferni's 600 cc record, made in August 1933.

The local 'school' again did well. J. Henry won the Experts Barred, and Handicap event in the Unlimited category, but unfortunately no details are given of his times, or what machine he used. It was most likely supercharged!

Basil Keys did not hang about either. He won the 350 cc Open class once more, and again broke the course record, the Norton needing only 13.26 seconds to complete the course! This again placed him with the Six Fastest Riders, and if it hadn't been for Frank Williams, he would have won that as well! As Frank nearly smashed the 600 cc record, Basil had to be content with second place on a 350!; even Francis Beart, Tom Pullin, S.H. Goddard and A. Leveson Gower, all Bemsee members, had to give way to the irrepressible Basil.

Yet a third meeting was held in 1938, the only year to see three. This was on 6th August and no less a celebrity than S 'Ginger' Wood turned up, with a 998 cc Vincent HRD Rapide. H. Trevor-Battye also arrived, with his old big twin Zenith. No records appear to have been broken, and Noel Pope's Brough made the best time of the day, to win the Bickell Cup in 11.87 seconds.

I recorded my fastest ever run on my 250 Excelsior in 16.91 seconds. This brought me into second place in the 250 Experts class, which was won by R.C.C. Palmer, in 15.98 seconds, on a similar machine.

This little 250, in spite of a very unfavourable power to weight ratio, (it was asked to take a far heavier jockey than Noel Pope's supercharged Brough!) gave me the only two firsts that I ever gained in sprint trials at Gatwick. I discovered the times were affected more by a rider's weight than at any other meeting, as being only quarter mile there was no chance to offset the effect of getting a heavier jockey on the move by flat out speed later on. This was well demonstrated by (1) Basil Keys, about the lightest rider there and (2) J. Lockett when he rode Francis Beart's Norton, as his times were well below what Francis had been able to do over several years; again he was much lighter than Francis. Eric Fernihough and myself were probably the heaviest of the regular jockeys, but Eric was mostly on his big Brough, the least affected.

Time was now rapidly out running for our enjoyable Saturday afternoons at Gatwick. The first meeting for the '39 season took place on 25th March and was notable for two things; a bitterly cold North-East wind, and Noel Pope with his new Brough Superior shattering Ferni's course record. Noel clocked 11.53 seconds, equal to 78.06 mph. This became the final course record and was never broken.

John Henry's 346 cc supercharged AJS in May 1938 *(J.H. Pigneguy)*

The wind, of course, did not help the speeds, so Noel's run was all the more remarkable.

Basil managed to win the 350 cc Open again, but in the slower time of 13.92 seconds. Second man was W.A. Lampkin, 348 cc Velocette, in 14.32 seconds. The latter was paying his first visit, with one of the new Velocettes, and had a regular field day.

For the Six Fastest, Noel Pope (Brough) and D.A. Loveday could not get their motors started owing to the cold, so the honours went to Francis Beart's Norton, in 13.25 seconds. Second was Frank William's elderly Cotton, now owned by R. London, in 13.56 seconds, and third Basil Keys on his 348 cc Norton, in 13.84 seconds.

I was awaiting the delivery of my new Ariel from Selly Oak, so I did not compete. I noted with satisfaction, however, that the Beart Trophy for consistency was won by V.S. Easter on a 497 cc Ariel, with 0.12 seconds variation between his four runs. This was exactly the same as my time the previous year, when I was only runner-up.

We now came to the end of the Gatwick story, only we did not know it at the time. The last of the pre-war series took place on 20th May 1939. Few people present could have known that it would be six years before racing could be even thought of, let alone resumed. Still less likely would anyone have dared to suggest that our dearly beloved speed trial course would be bulldozed into the huge confines of the new Gatwick Airport then, of course, not even under consideration.

For this last meeting we were treated to a bright sunny afternoon and a steady breeze blowing down the course this time, for a change. Just the day for records one old hand was heard to exclaim. Actually no records were broken, but no fewer than 10 riders were blown into the Experts class, myself being included in the 600 cc 'department' after 5 years!

Bemsee member J. Lockett, riding Francis Beart's Norton, became an Expert on his very first run, timed at 13.25 seconds, whilst Frank's old fire engine did the same for its new owner with a run in 13.18 seconds. Best of all, our local star J. Henry, now on a supercharged 500 cc Triumph twin, rocketed down in 12.92 seconds, to snatch the Experts Barred class from Locket by 1/100th of a second!

The latter discovered that he now had a split carburettor body, so was unable to run in the Handicap event. Frantic searching by the Beart camp produced another body from a non-competing machine. This was duly installed, and Lockett proceeded to win the Open class, and also to make fastest time of the day in 12.74 seconds, as Noel Pope's Brough could record only 12.87 seconds.

My own Ariel performed at this meeting, but being very new was not developed sufficiently to get amongst the rapid machinery present that day. However, it was very consistent, and once more I won the Beart Trophy for consistency, having only 0.11 seconds variation between my best four runs. *Motor*

Cycling reported '... in contrast to A.C. Perryman, whose 497 cc rear sprung Red Hunter Ariel went straight as a die and very fast.'

It did, however, get itself into the Six Fastest which J. Henry's Triumph won in 13.01 seconds. My time was 13.44 seconds. My four runs for the Beart Trophy were 13.54, 13.50, 13.43 and 13.44 seconds, the best giving 67.91 mph and the slowest 66.47 mph.

The old Ariel's cylinder base had been reduced by 1/8 in and compression plates were used to arrive at the required ratio. For Gatwick this had proved to be 12.96 to 1, with one thin plate. The new Ariel had a standard barrel, with the bronze head off the old model, which would give a compression ratio of approximately 11 to 1. This was a considerable reduction. Furthermore, Ariel No 2 had higher gear ratios on the three lower gears, as it was fitted with a Burman TT close ratio gearbox. There is no doubt in my mind that had I been able to continue to race, and modify it, it would have been very potent at Gatwick, and surpassed its predecessor.

Chapter Eight

The Brighton Speed Trials

After a lapse of many years, the Brighton and Hove Motor Club re-introduced the Speed Trials along the Brighton front, on 17th September 1932. A standing start half mile had been marked out along the Madeira Drive, a private road owned by Brighton Corporation. Why I was not present at this meeting is a mystery, but my records are a complete blank.

However, *The Motor Cycle* reports that R.W. Storey with his Brough Superior returned 24 4/5 seconds, 72.58 mph, and that from a push start. Later, from a clutch start, he clocked 22 1/5 secs., 81.08 mph, the first competitor ever to exceed 80 mph for this course. The fastest car, Sir Malcolm Campbell's supercharged 4 litre Sunbeam, returned 76.27 mph.

The next year, 23rd September 1933, the contestants included Eric Fernihough and, as was to be expected, his 344 cc Excelsior JAP won the 350 cc class at 65.69 mph in 27.4 seconds. His 498 cc sprint special of the same marque needed only 24.4 seconds, 73.77 mph.

The fastest car was Whitney Straight's Maserati, which took 24 1/5 seconds but the honours still rested with the bikes as Ron Storey took Barry's Brough down in 23 1/5 seconds, 77.59 mph.

The local press devoted most of their report space to the cars, and the feeling amongst the motorcycle brigade was that they were there under sufferance, looked upon as the poor relations. The public, however, always seemed to enjoy the bikes more as the latter returned higher speeds than all but the fastest cars. Some sports cars had a job to reach 40 mph in the smaller classes! The push starts of the first series seemed to have been abandoned for 1933 and onwards, in view of Fernihough's times.

For 1934 the meeting on 15th September had attracted entries from further afield, several riders from the North competing. Weather conditions were perfect, with a cloudless sky and no wind, and this was reflected in the higher speeds recorded. Ferni recorded 71.43 mph in winning the 350 cc class from Northerner R.F. Parkinson's AJS, which clocked 66.67 mph; local rider T.L. Beamish clocked 61.22 mph on A.G. Mitchell's 1932 TT Velocette, to finish fourth.

The 600 cc class was again taken by the irrepressible Eric Fernihough, his 498 cc Excelsior JAP increasing its winning speed to 77.59 mph, followed by the village fire engine, the 498 cc Cotton Blackburne of Frank Williams, which returned 74.38 mph. Frank's brother Leonard clocked 71.43 mph, with his 498 cc Scott.

So fast was the course this year that the first six in this class all bettered 70 mph, and the seventh man, R.C.C. Palmer, clocked 69.77 mph on his 490 cc Norton.

A most notable third place was annexed by Miss. T.E. Wallach on another 498 cc Excelsior JAP at 73.77 mph. She must have been the fastest lady in Brighton on that day!

The Unlimited Class, as everyone expected, went to Noel Pope, with his supercharged Brough, which increased its speed to 80.36 mph, almost 3 mph better than last year's. Without its silencers, Noel's machine had a voice that caused definite pain in the ears!

A very creditable speed of 69.23 mph was clocked by a friend of mine, Stuart Stubbings, on his then new twin port Red Hunter Ariel. He won the Brighton and Hove Member's class, whilst Tom Fassett, on the 348 cc Velocette that I was destined to acquire the following year, finished second in this class, at 64.75 mph.

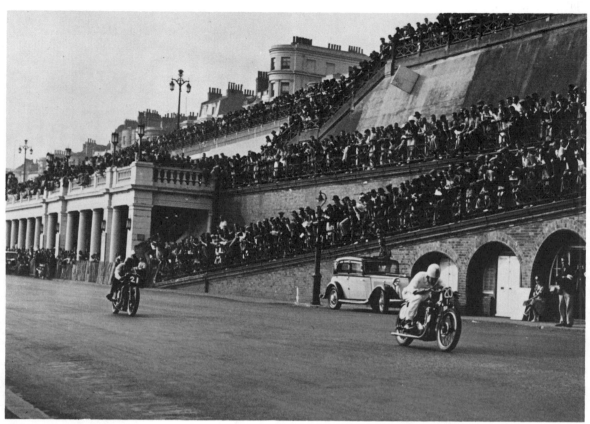

15th September 1934. Stuart Stubbings, 497 cc Ariel, winning the event for Brighton *(Motor Cycle)*

C.B. (Ben) Bickell taking second place in the Unlimited Sidecar Class at 68.70 mph in the Brighton Speed Trials 14th September 1935*(Motor Cycle)*

The last event was a Match Race between Noel Pope and R.O. Shuttleworth's 2,263 cc Bugatti, the fastest car. Unfortunately Noel oiled one of his plugs so that the car won at 75.63 mph against the 73.77 mph he could muster under the circumstances.

These speed trials had now become quite popular, so that on 14th September 1935 more Brooklands stars came along, including Ben Bickell with his supercharged Ariel four. Having established a 500 cc time last year that was well out of most people's reach, viz:- 77.59 mph, Eric left the 500 at home, exchanging it for his 246 cc Excelsior JAP, and again bringing his 350.

It was against his principle to attend a meeting and be unable to record the fastest time of the day however, so he had armed himself with his latest creation. And what a creation! A 996 cc Brough Superior which featured two 498 cc racing JAP engines on a common crankcase. He had raised the Brooklands Outer Circuit lap record to over 123 mph that very July of '35 with this machine, which was destined to shatter the course record **twice** that September afternoon.

As a curtain raiser, Eric trundled the 250 down the course at 65.22 mph, 6 mph faster than the second man, E.E. Garfield, on a 246 OK. JAP, and almost 8 mph faster than K.A. Frogley's 249 cc BSA.

He next unfurled the wrappings from the 344 cc model and annexed the 350 cc honours with that, at 68.70 mph, 4 mph faster than local rider Basil Keys, whose 348 cc Velocette returned a second place speed of 64.75 mph.

For the 600 c Solo Class, it was Ben's turn, Eric not having entered, and he treated the crowd to a glorious tune on his supercharged Ariel four, winning at 76.92 mph. Frank's fire engine and L.E. Good's 499 cc Rudge tied for second place at 73.17 mph, 2 1/2 mph down on last year's speed.

In the Unlimited Solos, Noel Pope was first on the line with the blown Brough. He made a perfect getaway, but his speed of 74.38 mph was 6 mph slower than his last year's performance, and not good enough to put him in the first three. Eric ran next, as the big fellows ran one at a time instead of in pairs, like the smaller fry. With the unleashing of all that power through one tyre, they were likely to charge about all over the place when starting.

This time Eric did not disappoint us! The speed he returned was 87.38 mph, shattering the course record by over 7 mph on a day when the course was not at its fastest. Ron Storey returned a very creditable 79.65 mph, and Ben's four pipped Noel for third place, at 76.92 mph.

In the Sidecar Class more records fell. Eric attached his sidecar and treated the crowd to another polished display. His speed was 75.00 mph, about 8 1/2 mph faster than that recorded by Barry, two years previous. Ben's Ariel four took second place, at 68.70 mph, an excellent speed this, and W.E. Bury took his 746 cc Douglas along to the tune of 67.16 mph. Stuart Stubbings repeated his performance of the previous year and clocked 68.70 mph on his Ariel.

Eric would not be satisfied until he had clocked that magic 90, and he got another chance in the special event of fastest car versus fastest motorcycle. The former was again R.O. Shuttleworth, this time with a 2,904 cc Alfa Romeo, which returned 79.36 mph. Eric improved on his previous speed, and although he did not realise his ambition, his 88.70 mph left the crowd in no doubt that it would be worth a visit next year, as Eric was the sort of man who was not to be denied any ambition that he cherished.

If anyone remembered Eric's near miss of the previous year, and there must have been a good many who did, they helped to swell the crowd on 26th September 1936. The morning was luckily given over to car racing, which was just as well, as the pitiless rain did not relent until lunch time. Several unkind riders blamed this on me, as for the first time in five years, my name appeared in the entry list! How I managed not to enter the previous four year's events, within six miles of my own doorstep, is one of the inexplicable lapses to which we are all suspect, I presume. I still cannot understand it. I could go 50 or 60 miles to Brooklands and grass tracks in Kent and Surrey, but not a few miles to Brighton. When I did arrive on the scene, I encountered the most wretched weather, instead of the glorious sunshine of some of the previous series. Although conditions did improve, the road was still wet when the sidecar outfits ran, causing them to leave clouds of spray in their wake as they rocketed down the course. Speeds were down yet again on the previous year, so no one expected anything spectacular.

The 250's started the cycle part of the proceedings, and in this Eric made one of his very few falls from grace; he missed a gear! This enabled my partner in business, W.R. (Bill) Beamish to win this heat (they were despatched in two's) on his 246 c New Imperial. Best time, however, was made by E.S.

Brighton Speed Trials 26th September 1936. Basil Keys gets ready to start on his 348 cc Velocette (36). No. 12 is a 348 cc Norton *(Motor Cycle)*

BRIGHTON AND HOVE MOTOR CLUB LTD.

SPEED   TRIALS   :   BRIGHTON.

This is to Certify that *The entry of Messrs Beamish Bro. on Ariel 497 c.c.*

driven by *A. C. Perryman*

attained an average speed of *70·90* m.p.h.

from a Standing Start, timed over half a mile.

R.A.C. Timekeeper

Sept 26 1936
Date

Hanley Chandler
Hon. Secretary of the Meeting

Another precious piece of paper, a certificate issued by the Brighton and Hove Motor Club showing the best speed recorded by each competitor

Chapman on his 249 cc Rudge at a speed of 54.88 mph, against Bill's second place at 54.71 mph. G. Tuffnell, 248 cc OK Supreme recorded 54.55 mph. Eric was not in the first three!

This was most un Ferni-like, to coin a phrase, but he made amends by taking the 344 cc model down at 67.92 mph, 3/4 mph slower than the previous year but still 3.17 mph faster than C.K. Mortimer's 348 cc Norton, in second place, at 64.75 mph.

It was the turn of the 600's to show their mettle, and Johnny Waite's Norton at 72.58 mph just pipped Frank Williams's 498 cc Cotton Blackburne at 72.29 mph. I filled third place by taking the Ariel down at 70.87 mph. Frank was 0.88 mph slower than the previous year, reflecting the slow state of the course.

Here would be an opportunity to record an amusing part of *The Motor Cycle* report, which gave us a laugh for some time to come! 'A.C. Perryman (497 Ariel) who had entered in the *Sidecar* events, but arrived after they had been run, took his sidecar off and rode in the solo class, collecting a third place for his trouble.' I had never handled a sidecar outfit in my life, and it was to be another five years hence before I did! Where the scribe got this from we never knew, but for months afterwards anyone enquiring after me when I was not available, usually evoked the quip 'I expect he's down on Brighton front, looking for that phantom sidecar he took off' It has never been found, even to this day!

To return to the day's events. Eric, determined not to be denied fastest time that year, had armed himself with **two** Brough Superiors, one supercharged and the unblown one he used the last year. He rode both in the Unlimited Solos class, the blown one recording 87.38 mph, and the unblown one 82.32 mph. Frank Williams collected third place with his Cotton at 73.17 mph exactly the same speed that he recorded the previous year. Evidently the course was improving!

In the Unlimited Sidecar Class Eric was first at 73.77 mph, whilst E.G. Bishop's 590 cc Excelsior JAP took the 600 cc honours at 62.94 mph.

The fastest car proved to be S.E. Cummings 2,998 cc supercharged Vauxhall Villiers, which had refused to motor after clocking 78.60 mph, causing the owner and car to return home.

The 90 bug was still gnawing away at Eric, so he wheeled out the unblown Brough to have another try on his own, without the car. He made a perfect getaway; there was only one tiny misfire halfway down the course, and the result was twenty seconds flat for the half mile, from a standing start, a speed of exactly 90 mph. **HE HAD DONE IT!**

25th September 1937 saw us once more on the Brighton front. My reception was quite hostile. 'Why the hell don't you keep away from the bloody place, we never got this bleeding rain till you decided to come along. It was always sunshine without you in the entries.' The only people to operate on dry roads this year were the sidecars. All the solo classes had to contend with wet roads and miserable conditions.

Eric must have known what was in store; he hadn't bothered to enter! Francis Beart came along this time instead, bringing a 499 cc supercharged Douglas with him, to collect the 600 cc Sidecar honours at 65.57 mph, and the Unlimited at 64.80 mph. Second place each time was taken by E.V. Evans with a 498 cc OEC outfit. None of the Brough brigade had turned up, wise chaps!

Charles Mortimer was again successful with his 348 cc Norton at the improved speed of 67.04 mph, about 2 1/2 mph faster than his second place time of the previous year. W.A. Lampkin brought his 348 cc Velocette into second place, ahead of local rider J. Henry on his 346 cc AJS; again no speeds were recorded.

In the 600 cc Class, history repeated iteself. Johnny Waite could not coax any more than 70.87 mph out of his Norton, but he still beat Frank's Cotton (no speed recorded). I filled third place once again with the Ariel, with a mere 69.58 mph.

In the Unlimited Class, Johnny was again the winner with the enhanced speed of 73.20 mph and I managed to finish second at 70.45 mph. T. Arter on a 495 cc AJS took third place. This was to prove the very last event in which I would ride my old faithful Ariel.

No doubt because of the poor weather conditions of the last two September meetings, the organisers switched the 1938 event to 2nd July, in the hope of some sunshine. But they had reckoned without my power of attracting foul weather, and the morning was graced with an honest to goodness downpour, with a thunderstorm thrown in for good measure!

The only motorcycle class run in the morning was the 250 cc and I was due to take part in this very class with my 249 cc Excelsior Manxman. There were only four of us in this class, and although the rain had ceased by the time we took the field, the road was still wet. R.C.C. Palmer's Excelsior returned 31.17 seconds, 57.75 mph against my 32.67 seconds, and 55.10 mph. E.S. Chapman on his 249 cc Rudge was third, in 33.60 seconds, 53.57 mph, 1 1/2 mph slower than when he won this class in 1936.

The scribe reporting this recorded Palmer's time, and then went on 'A.C. Perryman on a similar machine, could do no better than 32.67 seconds, but judging by his pedalling act when getting away, his Excelsior was overgeared.' I had learnt this escapade from a very successful 250 cc exponent at the Gatwick Speed Trials and his theory was that anything you could do with physical effort to help these little 'uns off the mark was well worth it, seeing that you were being timed to 1/100 of a second. I was using only petrol in my cycle, so I did not expect the same results as those from the alcohol motors like Eric Fernihough's and others. In addition, I thought that a little manual effort would not be out of place to assist my little 250 off the mark, with my not inconsiderable weight!

On handing me this 250 in the Isle of Man, Ginger Wood's instructions were 'She peaks at 7350 giving you a good 22 horses. Keep your revs around 7000, but if they drop much below this, change down, as around 6600 the valve springs are liable to break.' This machine was fitted with triple coil valve springs, each one inside its larger neighbour.

I found from my own experience that when starting in bottom, even getting over the 7000 rpm mark before letting in the clutch, the revs would come right down to about the 3000 mark, upon getting off the line. The acceleration then was poor, until the rev-counter reached 4500. Then things happened. The motor became alive, the exhaust note changed completely, and it felt as if someone had kicked you violently in the back.

This was the real reason for my pedalling act, to help the little motor up to the 4500 rpm mark. It had nothing to do with being overgeared. Machines fitted with megaphone exhaust systems have similar characteristics, but the Excelsior had only a plain open pipe. Once under way, everything was fine, but valuable seconds must have been sacrificed at the start.

Anyway, for some reason that I have now forgotten, poor Palmer was disqualified by the Stewards. Maybe he had jumped the lights at the start, and my pedalled Excelsior was adjudged the class winner.

It was useless for me to enter any other class with my 250, and in view of the weather conditions, and the ribbing I was getting from my fellow riders for bringing it with me, I loaded up the bike and made tracks for home.

Brighton Speed Trials, 2nd July 1938. The Author winning the 250 cc class on his 248 cc Excelsior Manxman *(James Brymer)*

Reading the account of the rest of the programme, I wish I had stayed, as my old colleague of so many past scraps, Frank Williams, had a veritable field day with his fire engine. He won the 600 cc Solos, the Unlimited ditto, and the Handicap events. Nice going Frank!

In the Unlimited Class, local rider J. Henry had **SUPERCHARGED** J.J.G. Hempson's 990 cc side-valve AJS and just failed to catch Francis when he recorded 59.80 mph. Unsupercharged, this outfit had won the Sidecar Class at Gatwick in April 1938 and John, being in the Experimental Department of Ricardos, earning his daily bread amongst the blowers, applied his expertise to this side-valve job. The next year he gave his new Triumph twin the same treatment, considerably enhancing its performance.

Another local rider to achieve fame was Basil Keys, on one of Noel Pope's 348 cc Nortons that he had acquired and breathed on. Not content with breaking the 350 cc course record at Gatwick with it, Basil now proceeded to win the 350 class this day, and break Ferni's course record made 4 years previously by almost 1 mph. As if this was not enough, he motored so well in the 600 cc event that he gained second place to Frank Williams's fire engine, increasing his 350 cc class speed by another 1/2 mph. This was even better than Francis Beart could manage on his bored out 502 cc job, who had to be content with third place.

Frank Williams, living in Rottingdean, probably nearer the course than any other competitor, also was classed as a local rider, although he was not strictly in our local school. I have already listed his bag for the day, and in winning the Handicap at a speed of 77.52 mph, he came within 0.04 mph of Ferni's 500 cc course record!

The locals had virtually swept the board at this meeting, and at the finish were responsible for:-

250 cc Class - First A.C. Perryman.
350 cc Class - First B.E. Keys.
600 cc Class - First and Second F.J. Williams and B.E. Keys.
Unlimited Solos - First F.J. Williams.
Handicap - First F.J. Williams.
Unlimited Sidecars - Second J. Henry.

All of these riders were regular performers at Brooklands so it was also a triumph for the BMCRC, Francis Beart filling in the gaps above. Also, of course, Basil's Norton had broken the 350 cc course record.

Whether it was coincidence or not is impossible to say. Certainly with my departure after the 250 class the weather must have improved, or the speeds would not have been so high. But Brighton had never been a happy hunting ground for me, like Gatwick.

Even at this early stage, I had made up my mind that I would not be on a 250 next year. If possible, I would get another Ariel. Then I could have another go at Frank's fire engine!

Fate decreed otherwise. I got the Ariel, and the event was to have been on 24th September. The second World War broke out on 3rd September however, so the event was never held.

The 1938 event proved to be the last of the pre-war series. By the time the post-war series resumed, I had retired from the racing scene. The events are still held today. The speeds attained and the machines used bear no resemblance to those of my day. I doubt if the competitors will enjoy themselves as much as we did, in those pre-war days. One very happy thought though. Basil Keys still rides there, and wins! He now uses a Norton frame housing a 996 cc JAP engine and has returned 108 mph. He also has a supercharged version that he is still playing with.

In a lighter vein at this last meeting, a 1901 ARIEL tricycle was piloted down the course in 63.50 seconds by E. Marshall. *The Motor Cycle* report of the meeting also states that Basil Keys broke the 350 cc course record with a time of **24 minutes 87 secs!** Basil thinks that even if he had slipped the clutch in bottom gear, he would not have been able to take as long as that, with the return journey thrown in as well! Obviously those early scribes could not have checked their records very thoroughly.

Chapter Nine
The Final Year

Although I had experienced a quite successful season, with reliability rather than speed the keynote, I yearned to be back on something with a bit more urge than my 250 was capable of unleashing. Thoughts immediately went back to my old friend, the Ariel single port, particularly as the firm had evolved a spring frame for 1939. Accordingly, I had a word with the Service Manager of Ariels at the 1938 Motor Cycle Show, as by now I was on very friendly terms with him, and indeed, with the firm as a whole. It was agreed that they would build me a machine for racing, using standard parts, but incorporating such alterations as I wished, to render the job more suitable for differing conditions.

Such things as clutch and brake levers, which had given me trouble by breakage on the old job, I specified in the schedule 'As on Excelsior'. In all, probably more than a dozen items were so listed, and when I went to the works later to inspect it at their request, Ernie Smith Chief of the Experimental Department told me that my specification had almost caused a strike! 'Why didn't he buy a bloody Excelsior?' was the universal comment.

Anyway, as we were Ariel agents, the order went through in the usual way, and an ordinary product came off the production line to be wheeled straight into the Experimental Department. Here the motor was removed and stripped completely. Ernie Smith then carefully went over it, rebuilding it with loving care and fitting the TT 36 carburettor (light alloy type) and Lucas racing magneto that I had specified. It was also furnished with the 1935 type of head and rocker box, not the 1938 type with enclosed valve springs and push rod tubes going into the head itself. I still had the bronze head off my old favourite on which a lot of loving care had been lavished, and I hoped to use it on this new engine. Hence the old type of cast iron head was fitted at the works. A 'loch ness monster', as the Excelsior lads had called the racing saddle, was fitted instead of a road type and the complete oilbath chaincase had been discarded in favour of an alloy guard over the top run of the chain. The clutch linings and springs were also changed for those of the racing variety. A four-speed Burman close ratio gearbox was substituted for the standard article. Brake linings, of course, were changed to the Ferodo MZ grade, so that little remained of the standard machine. The oil pressure gauge pipe had been taken round to the rear of the cylinder base, as I had done on the previous engine, and the standard petrol tank had been put back in the stores to make way for the very neat, narrow type, as used by Jock West on his Hartley Ariel. A 250 cc fork spring was also substituted for the standard type. Up till then the maximum brake horse power extracted from this type of engine was 30 bhp; this was so in the case of the one used by Len Heath in the International Six Day's Trial.

After they had finished my engine it was tested, and it returned 32 bhp, so the works were well satisfied with it. These figures, of course, related to running on 50/50 petrol-benzol mixture. The camshaft used was the standard type, not the special valve spring buster that I had used in the old engine.

Owing to the movement of the rear springing, the pivot for the rear brake pedal had to be at the

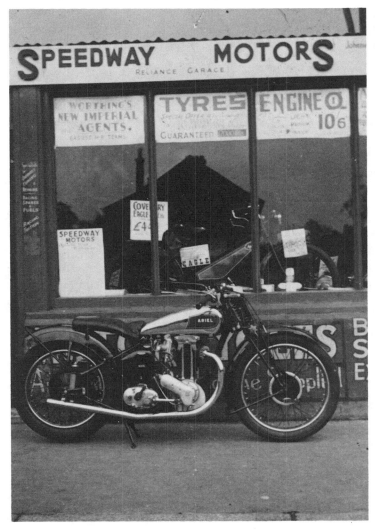

Ariel No. 3, specially built at Selly Oak taken on arrival at the Author's place of business, West Worthing, in May 1939

centre of the geometry of the spring heel. When using standard touring footrests, the end of the long brake pedal was in the correct position, under the rider's toe. The racing footrests that I was to use, of course, were to be further to the rear, and as the pedal's fulcrum could not be moved, the operation of the rear brake presented a problem, which the dear works passed over to yours truly!

To make matters worse, the firm in which I was a partner had passed into the hands of the Official Receiver, and I had to instruct the works to cease operations for the time being. Luckily, I was not long on the shelf as I managed to secure a post with a local speedway enthusiast, running a garage business in West Worthing. I notified the works of the change and the job proceeded once more, the now completed Ariel being sent on the passenger train to West Worthing station, just along the road. The racer was on view outside the shop for the rest of the day, and it created great interest and speculation. By the time I had evolved a cable-operated rear brake system, the season had already got under way, and I had missed several meetings.

However, everything was now ready, so it was to the Brooklands Road Championship meeting on 13th May that the new model was transported for its introduction to Weybridge, and its first outing. This, of course, was scheduled to take place on the Campbell Circuit, where the entire events that afternoon were to be run.

The start was extremely rapid, the first right-hander being not far from the start. I soon realised that the braking system was anything but adequate, and that unless the front brake on its own could reduce our headlong rush, disaster was imminent. The model was already leaned over for the swervery, and the extra demanded from that front brake did the rest. There was a sickening lurch, which I managed to correct, then the whole equipage subsided rapidly, and decanted yours truly in the dust. The lion's share of the impact was absorbed by my right shoulder, the Ariel being virtually undamaged. After retrieving the model from its horizontal position adjacent to the barrier, I restored it to the vertical and resumed operations.

It was hopeless. I had no confidence in the brakes and my shoulder was hurting like blazes. I found I was shutting off much earlier than usual, to be sure of not resuming a horizontal position, and was most relieved eventually to get the chequered flag. I decided to call it a day, packed up and went home.

The Ariel's next outing was on 24th June, this time running on alcohol fuel. When I had entered for two five lap Mountain handicap races I had requested the Secretary to send through my lap times, and I see that my best lap was the last one in the second race - 69.04 mph. There was still the same uncertainty with the braking, and the first lap of the second race was the occasion of the unscheduled trip up the slip road, mentioned in Chapter two. My lap times were also erratic, showing a variation of eight seconds. It was obvious that the braking would have to be improved before it would even be as good as its predecessor.

I could not get the leverage I needed for that rear brake, as I have already recorded that the fulcrum was so far forward, and could not be moved. I managed to make a slight modification though, which I tried out during its next outing on 15th July, Mountain Championship Day. In its present condition it was quite useless to enter the Ariel for the twenty five lap Senior Championship, so I had to be content with the sole five lap handicap of the day. Here I had twenty five seconds start from Ron Harris on scratch and even fifteen seconds start on my old friend Dennis Loveday, with his Ariel. There was certainly an improvement this time and my second lap was the Ariel's best ever – fifty eight seconds, equivalent to 72.62 mph, which exactly equalled the best lap of its predecessor. The other laps, however, were nothing to write home about and I finished nowhere.

This meeting proved to be the last that would ever be staged at the famous track. The Brooklands Grand Prix of 23rd September and the Hutchinson Hundred of 21st October were never held, as the gathering war clouds burst over Europe on 3rd September 1939. So the development of my specially

A record of the lap times recorded during a Brooklands meeting, which was available to all competitors

Long distance events demanded a more elaborate record of lap times, as this form will show

In the Paddock at Brooklands on July 1939. J. Henry with his supercharged Triumph twin *(J.H. Pigneguy)*

The line up in the Paddock for the 10 lap Mountain race on 24th June 1939. The leading Velocette (14) belongs to R. Fazan, (10) is J.A. Peck, 498 cc OEC JAP, and (3) Francis Beart, 502 cc Norton. Noel Pope stands in front of the Norton in the light raincoat *(Motor Cycle)*

RON HARRIS

"The Rider Agent"

for your

REAL RACER, TOURER or SPORTS MACHINE

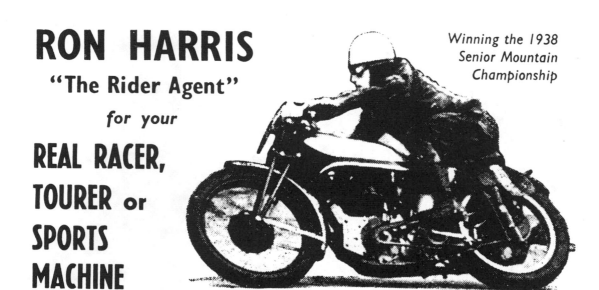

Winning the 1938 Senior Mountain Championship

Distributor : Norton — Triumph — Rudge — B.S.A.— Morgan

Holder : 500 c.c. and 750 c.c. Mountain Course Records

Winner :
1938 Senior Mountain Championship, Viscount Wakefield Trophy, etc.

Note the number of machines competing at this Meeting bearing my transfer

---

My Showrooms are open from 9 a.m. to 9 p.m. and are packed (door to door) with used and shop-soiled bargains from 90/- to £90. Lists by return if you cannot call.

My famous Adjustable Drip-Feed Terms over 6, 12, 18 or 24 months now include Personal Accident Cover—if you are incapacitated through an accident, whether on your machine or not, your payments are made for you.

RON HARRIS

"The Rider Agent"

KING ST., MAIDENHEAD

Also Depot at Brooklands Track

Immediate Delivery on all Models and a Real Rider-to-Rider Deal

Telephone
MAIDENHEAD 1271

Another advertisement from a Brooklands programme, in this instance relating to a 'Rider Agent'. Ron Harris was a very well known rider at the track, with a whole string of successes to his credit

This 249 cc radial valve Rudge won the first 5 lap Mountain Handicap for D.H. Whitehead at the last ever meeting held on 15th July 1939 *(Motor Cycle)*

The centrifugal supercharger on Miss B. Shilling's 490 cc Norton. The rider is G.A. Naylor who gained his Gold Star on it. Photographed on 24th June 1939 *(Motor Cycle)*

In the Paddock at Brooklands on 24th June 1939. The Author is on the works Ariel and John Henry is on his supercharged Triumph Speed Twin

Noel Pope unsuccessfully tried to beat the lap record on 24th June 1939 when his front piston tightened up. But his supercharged 996 cc Brough Superior gained it on Wednesday 5th July 1939 with a lap at 124.51 mph, the fastest ever recorded *(Motor Cycle)*

built racer ceased. Given time, I would certainly have overcome the braking problems, and I think that ultimately it would have proved an excellent job. Its handling was good and the motor could certainly turn out the horses. Instead it was converted back to standard. The works sent all the parts by post, and I fitted a low compression piston of 6 to 1 ratio to render it suitable for Pool petrol.

In June of the following year, Connie and I married, and the machine was used to transport the bride on its pillion, with me doing the navigation from the church. It would be interesting to know how many Brooklands racers ever did duty as a bridal carriage! Later the same year, as we were getting our home together under the difficult war conditions, it was called upon, in solo form, to transport a 6 foot roll of linoleum tied along the side of it, the shop's own transport having ceased owing to the war.

In common with most other people at that time, my services were required to further the war effort, in the shape of installing and maintaining machinery engaged in the production of gun mountings, and torpedo engine parts. My hours were long and erratic, and my racer had to get me to and fro. I lived about six miles from the factory, and also had to be there at night for fire watching duties, and later on, as Chief of the Fire Brigade.

We had some nasty spells of frost and snow, and a colleague who relied on a 600 cc Panther suggested that I emulate him and attach a sidecar for the winter months. Dan stated that so equipped, I would be able to cope with any weather conditions; a sidecar outfit being the best vehicle on the road, when ice and snow prevailed.

Ariels marketed their own triangulated sidecar chassis, and I cast around for one of these. On one of my trips home to visit my parents, I found one hanging up in a back street dealer's place. It was a chassis only, sans body; but I acquired same, and it was soon attached to the Ariel, on the premises. With Connie on the pillion I soon discovered that a bodyless sidecar outfit was anything but a desirable acquisition, especially on left-hand corners! We arrived safely at my parent's home, more by luck than anything else, but it was a near thing with a wall on the offside of one left-hander. This seemed to radiate a magnetic field towards the Ariel, and looked decidedly unyielding; at the last moment I won the battle and regained the correct side of the highway.

In view of this experience, I decided that some sort of ballast would need to be attached to that chassis, if we were to reach Burnham, Bucks, that night, sound in wind and limb. My fond father evolved the solution. He had on the premises a large, old, Victorian metal steamer trunk, that was slowly decaying. The lid was ripped off, and after fitting a conveniently handy plank of wood across the body supports of the chassis, the trunk was installed thereon with the aid of a few bolts.

I surveyed the creation with suspicion; it did not of itself solve the problem, as there was still need for some additional deterrent to that lifting sidecar wheel. Senior again was my salvation. 'Why not fill that trunk with coal' he jokingly suggested. 'That's it! We're very short of it, and you have an abundant stock' was my reply. So I set to work with a will, and the shovel soon had the best part of a couple of hundredweights of Derby Brights ensconced in the trunk. Several old sacks, suitably moistened from the water can were laid along the open top of the ensemble, to deter the dust from invading the atmosphere in Connie's vicinity.

In my apprenticeship days I had often heard the phrase, 'it's just like putting a racehorse in a coal cart' used to describe the lethargic progress of some unfortunate quadruped that had failed to live up to its reputation, and relieved the luckless punter of his stake monies. As with the bridal carriage, it would be interesting to know how many Brooklands racers were installed in a coal cart. It really was a case of Ben Bickell's Bickell JAP (ex-Chater Lea) in reverse! We duly resumed our rightful places on this equipage and reached our goal without further incident.

I had already been offered a two seater body locally, which had once been attached to a big twin BSA. This was now acquired, and with a little modification installed on the triangulated chassis. One other refinement was later added. A rectangular metal, all welded box, the shape of a large book, was installed in the nose, and supplied with hot air from the Ariel's exhaust pipe via a length of flexible tubing. The box also had an exhaust pipe to enable a continuous flow of hot gasses to circulate through it. The flexible pipe could be disconnected and a blank cap nut installed on the main exhaust pipe, when the outside temperature allowed it.

Connie made up a new hood for it, and when this was raised the degree of comfort was enhanced. So much so, that on several night journeys home from my parent's home, with our little mongrel terrier

During the 5 lap Mountain Handicap Race of the meeting held on 15th July 1939, A. Leveson-Gower, 490 cc Norton (16), G.E. Gott, 499 cc Vincent HRD (17) and W.A. Lampkin, 348 cc Velocette (18), round the Members Hill turn *(Motor Cycle)*

R.F. Hill, 348 cc plunger frame Norton (23), leads B.W. Smith, 344 cc OK Supreme JAP (24), into the Members Hill turn during the 5 lap Mountain Handicap Race of 15th July 1939 *(Motor Cycle)*

In the Junior Mountain Championship of 15th July 1939 last year's winner, H.C. Lamacraft (25) rides his 348 cc Velocette into second place, vainly chased by J.M. Givons on an older Velocette. This photograph is taken at the Members Hill turn *(Motor Cycle)*

During the Senior Mountain Championship of 15th July 1939, three Velocettes leave the fork turn. The riders are V.H. Willoughby (7), H.C. Lamacraft (8) and L.A. Dear (9) *(Motor Cycle)*

The Senior Mountain Championship of 15th July 1939 proved to be the last motorcycle race to be held at Brooklands. In this event, Johnny Lockett (15), riding Francis Beart's bored-out 502 cc Norton, leaves the fork turn to win. He is a lap ahead of three 348 cc Velocettes ridden by V.H. Willoughby (7), L.A. Dear (9) and H.C. Lamacraft (18) *(Motor Cycle)*

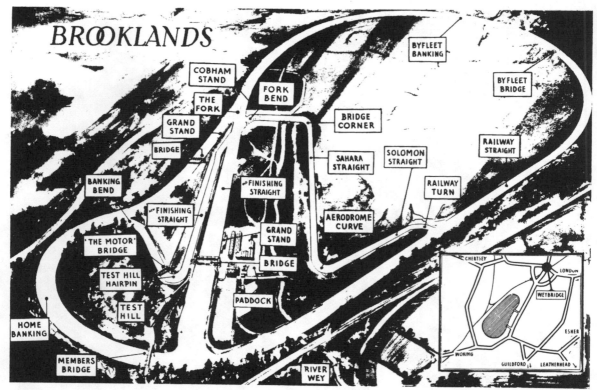

A sketch of Brooklands as it existed just prior to the outbreak of war during September 1939
(*Brooklands Society*)

down by her feet and the heater, the pair of them would drop off to sleep, leaving me to navigate on deserted roads, out in the cold night air!

The outfit with its two seater body proved its worth. There had been a particularly heavy snowfall one night, and all transport, including the Great Western Railway, was inoperative. Two other works employees, one of whom used the railway and the other a push bike, made their way to my house that morning. Our combined efforts resulted in the outfit gaining the public highway, and with one on the pillion to aid wheelgrip, and the other in the sidecar, we set out. About a mile from the works there was a right-hand bend. The snow had drifted over everything, leaving a completely level white sea. Unable to distinguish the path of the highway, I found without warning that we were halted by a solid wall of snow about five feet deep. The crew disembarked, and by our combined efforts we managed to extricate our outfit, rejoin the public highway, and ultimately reach the works. We were among the very few to reach the works that morning, the railway not operating until late morning, and road transport not until the following day.

Another incident in the snow is also worth recording. During the winter of 1940-41, if I was lucky enough to get a day off from the works, Connie and I took the opportunity to go down to Shoreham on the Ariel to visit my parents. We had not as yet acquired the sidecar, but although there had been some snow in Southern England, conditions in our locality were not too bad and it appeared reasonable that nearer the coast they should tend to improve.

We set out full of confidence, and all went well for some time. However, when nearing Horsham it was obvious that the snowfall had been heavier, and that conditions had become worse. Once we turned South on to the A24, there was a quite steep hill to be negotiated. Very little traffic was about in those days, mostly service vehicles. Well, the snow on this hill had been well and truly rolled down hard, most likely by army lorries, and as I approached I could see it had a shiny surface like glass. About halfway up the hill was an army despatch rider on a side-valve Norton, broadside across the road and unable to ascend by any means known to him. Realising that I would be in a similar predicament if I tried to climb

Noel Christmas after winning the Hutchinson Hundred on his 348 cc Velocette at 97.46 mph on 28th September 1935 *(Motor Cycle)*

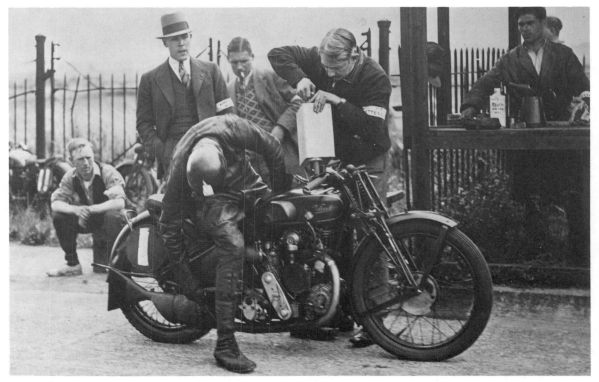

Harold Willis's 348 cc supercharged Velocette 'Whiffling Clara' being refuelled by J.A. (Pa) Archer in the Junior Grand Prix of 23rd July 1932. L.J. (Les) Archer is the rider and he finished 3rd in the Junior and 2nd in the Senior on this machine. *(Motor Cycle)*

Ivan Wicksteed raised the 500 cc Outer Circuit record to 118.02 mph with M. Winslow's 496 cc supercharged Triumph twin on 8th October 1938 *(Motor Cycle)*

H.C. Lamacraft's supercharged 348 cc Velocette in the Paddock at Brooklands on 12th March 1938 *(Motor Cycle)*

as he had, I suddenly remembered my old trials techniques, and telling Connie to hang on, I diverted the Ariel onto the grass verge on the near side. Here was virgin snow, on top of rough grass; the sprung rear wheel took care of the uneven terrain, and the Ariel sailed up as if it were on a dry road.

The look of astonishment on the face of the DR as we passed him at about 20 mph was a source of amusement to us for the rest of the day. From then on we spent more time on the grass verge than we did on the road surface proper! But it worked, and we arrived safely at our goal.

On many occasions other road users were in for a shock when they tried to pass us, either solo or sidecar. The Ariel would still do about 85 mph solo. After the war, having decided to discontinue racing, I sold it, so that I might acquire a car for my business. The new owner refitted the original piston, as by this time higher octane value fuel was available, permitting the increased compression ratio. This still further increased the performance, and so it passed into other spheres of activity.

The special accessories that had graced the two Ariels, eg. the bronze head, racing magneto, special cam, special tank etc., etc., I disposed of to that ace of Ariel tuners, L.W.E. Hartley of Plumstead. The latter, of course, specialised in producing very rapid examples of this marque, and with hindsight, I regret that I never enlisted his aid in rebalancing my own engine. He would most likely have enhanced still further its performance.

It is conceivable that some of the parts of my beloved Ariel formed part of the anatomy of various machines that Laurence was responsible for, thus continuing to uphold Ariel prestige.

And so my glorious 8 years of motorcycle racing came to an end on Saturday 15th July 1939, Mountain Championship Day at Brooklands. There was never any motorcycle events at the track during August and, of course, the horror of the Second World War burst upon us on September 3rd. Not only the racing ceased. The famous track itself suffered through enemy action. Great gaping holes were torn in its surface, accompanied by tragic loss of life amongst Vickers' personnel.

The man who travelled faster than anyone else at Brooklands, E.C. Fernihough, who covered the flying kilo at 143.39 mph on 12th March 1938 with a maximum speed of 158 mph as he crossed the line. He is seen here on his 996 cc supercharged Brough Superior in the condition it was in on its ill-fated attack on the world speed record on 23rd April 1938 *(Motor Cycle)*

Guy Newman, a consistent performer, on his Mark V 348 cc Velocette, established a 5 lap Mountain record on 25th June 1938 *(Motor Cycle)*

Ron Harris, holder of the 500 cc 5 lap Mountain course record, on 17th July 1937 *(Motor Cycle)*

F.W.S. Clarke won a 3 lap handicap race on this 249 cc Triumph at 92.06 mph, with a lap at 97 mph on 12th March 1938 *(Motor Cycle)*

12th March 1938. L.J. Archer, 348 cc Velocette (3), swings round the outside of H.C. Lamacraft, Velocette (5), on the Test Hill hairpin of the Campbell Circuit *(Motor Cycle)*

When the guns were at last silenced in Europe in May 1945, we were in a very different world from the balmy days of the 1930's. No one could forsee how long it would be before racing returned, or indeed what form it would take. I knew my favourite track would never see racing again, and now married, with the birth of my first child imminent, I decided that the most sensible thing would be to say 'au revoir' to what had been a very enjoyable period of my life.

I have several times been asked by motorcyclists of today what stands out most in my mind of my Brooklands experiences. I think the palm must surely go to the amazing start of Leonard Williams' extraordinary Scott two-stroke, in the two lap Outer Circuit race at Clubman's Day in 1935. With foot poised on the kickstarter as Secretary Duncan Ferguson held his starter's flag aloft, Leonard brought his foot down in line with that flag and the Scott was actually running by the time the flag fell. An equally rapid engagement of gear, with smart clutch work, and the Scott was just receding into the distance whilst the rest of us had only just started to push! That start alone must have given Leonard a bonus of at least 300 yards on all the rest. I have never seen anything like it before or since, and I can hear that glorious engine even now shattering the silence, when the only other sound came from shuffling feet!

A few words now about the awards. It may come as something of a shock to the racers of today, who are used to winning many thousands of pounds in a season's racing, not to mention the support they receive from their sponsors, to learn of our awards.

The Clubmen's awards consisted of silver cups and tankards, whilst Bemsee members for a three lap Outer Circuit, or a five lap Mountain race collected £3 3s for a first place, £1 11 6d for a second place, and 15s for a third. Cups could be taken in lieu of cash, if preferred; you had to state this on the entry form. For a ten lap Mountain race these figures were increased to £5 for first, £2 10s for second and £1 5s for third place.

The longer and more important races usually had a cup and cash, and the best of all, of course, was the Hutchy with its £200 Mellano Trophy, presented by Mr. A.V. Mellano. In addition Messrs. E.B. Meyrowitz Ltd., presented a pair of their famous No 12 *Luxor* Goggles to members gaining a Gold Star.

Finally there were the aggregate Cups for most points in 250 cc class, 350 cc, Unlimited cc, Passenger class, and the highest total of marks in all classes.

There is now good news for admirers of the old Brooklands. The Brooklands Society Ltd., held their 11th Annual reunion at the old track on 25th June 1978. I was present at this having joined the Society. It was good to see the old track again after forty years, and once more hear that gorgeous sound emenating from those silencers.

The Society hopes to acquire forty acres of the old site, which includes the old Clubhouse, Paddock, and many of the historic buildings flanking this nerve centre of the old track. Parts of the Campbell Circuit and Member's Banking are also included, and it is hoped to create a living museum of the activities which made Brooklands famous.

It is most unlikely that racing will ever take place again, but ex-track cars and motorcycles may be demonstrated, and non-speed events such as Driving Tests could be held.

The map of Brooklands as it was in 1939 is reproduced by courtesy of the Brooklands Society Ltd., and Mick Woollett, Editor of *Motor Cycle Weekly*.

Index

125

127